The Photographer's Weekend Book

Ex Libris

The Photographer's Weekend Book

101 Creative Projects for the Amateur Photographer

Michael Busselle

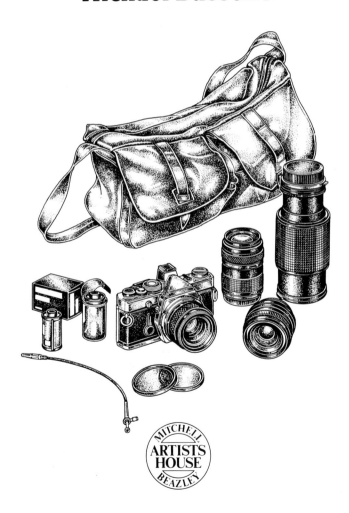

MITCHELL
ARTISTS
HOUSE
BEAZLEY

Contents

An Adkinson Parrish Book

First published in 1982 by
Mitchell Beazley Artists House
An imprint of Mitchell Beazley London Limited
Artists House 14-15 Manette Street
London W1V 5LB

ISBN 0 86134 033 7

Copyright © 1982 Adkinson Parrish Limited

Designed and produced by
Adkinson Parrish Limited, London

Managing Editor
Clare Howell

Editor
Hilary Dickinson

Art Editor
Christopher White

Designer
Martin Atcherley

Illustrators
Rick Blakely Phil Holmes Hayward Art Group

Composition in Photina by
Filmtype Services Limited,
Scarborough, North Yorkshire

Colour illustrations originated by
East Anglian Engraving Ltd, Norwich

Printed by Hazell Watson & Viney Limited
Aylesbury, Bucks

Introduction 6

Camera Techniques
Focusing effects 8
Using mirrors 10
Using coloured lights 12
Flash effects 14
Projector effects 16
Polarized light 18
Strobe effects 20
Ultra-violet light 22
Painting with light 24
False colour effects 26
Glass montage 28
Back projection 30
Tri-colour
    photographs 32
Using grain effects 34
Double exposure 36
Infra-red film 38
Using blur 40
Freezing movement 42
Exposure effects 44
Filters for dramatic
    black and white 46
Time exposures 48

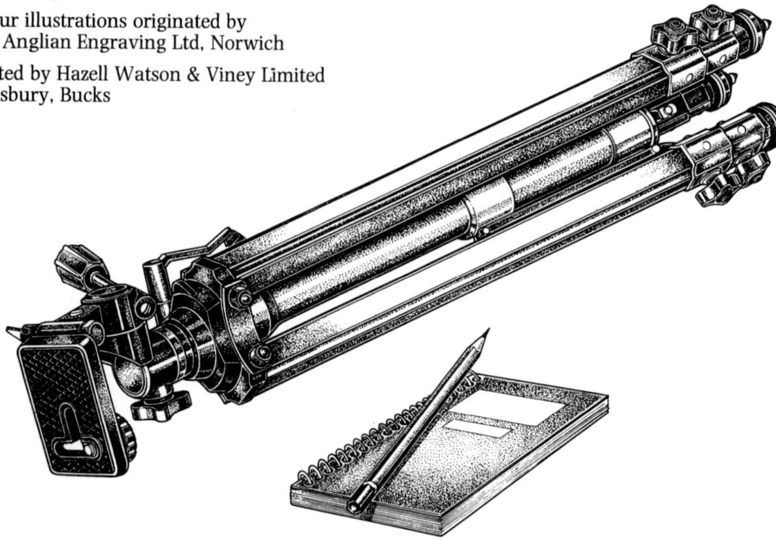

Subject Idea File
Neighbourhood safari 52
City lights 54
Food 56
Trees 58
The urban landscape 60
Junk objects 62
Shop windows 64
Reflected images 66
Street life 68
Animal portraits 70
People at work 72
Harbours 74
The zoo 76
The seaside 78
A children's
   playground 80
The races 82
The market 84
The park 86
Railways 88
The farm 90
Waterways 92
Industry 94
The circus 96

Style and Approach
A touch of humour 100
Bad weather 102
Using shadows 104
Romantic glamour 106
Framing the image 108
Heads in close-up 110
Silhouettes 112

Bird's-eye view 114
Photographic
   patterns 116
Using colour for
   mood 118
High-key
   photographs 120
Creating a sense
   of touch 122
Worm's-eye view 124
Keeping it simple 126
Low-key photographs 128
Bold colour effects 130
Shooting against
   the light 132
A picture story 134
The wide-angle
   approach 136
Architectural details 138
The telephoto
   approach 140
Nature in close-up 142

Special Assignments
Dramatic skies 146
Abstract nudes 148
Instant art 150
Shooting a
   picture series 152
Sunsets 154
A contact sheet
   mosaic 156
Making a flick book 158
A panoramic
   photograph 160

Shooting a step-by-step
   sequence 162
Illustrative
   photography 164
Making calendars
   and greetings cards 166
Using simple optics 168
Physiograms 170
A print portfolio 172
Photographs for
   decor 174
Snowscapes 176
Recording a holiday 178
A photo-essay 180

**Manipulating the
Image**
Tone separation 184
Texture screens 186
Solarized prints 188
Montage prints 190
Photograms 192
Line-sketch prints 194
Distorted prints 196
Print patterns 198
Hand-coloured prints 200
Collage 202
Making a slide
   sandwich 204
High-contrast effects 206
Making duplicate
   transparencies 208
Printing on
   different surfaces 210
Gum bichromate
   prints 212
Hand-made
   negatives 214
Toning black and
   white prints 216

Bibliography 218
Index 219
Acknowledgements 223

Introduction

Photography means many different things to different people; to some it is a means of self-expression, to others a means of earning a living, to others again a way of making a record of places and events. For the amateur photographer, however, photography should above all be a source of enjoyment, a leisure-time pursuit that can stimulate, infuriate, be totally absorbing, or while away an odd hour.

This book aims to fulfil at least some of the needs of everyone who owns, or is thinking of owning, a camera and, in addition, to suggest ways of extending the pleasure that you are already experiencing from a unique and rewarding hobby. Although the process of taking photographs is itself a pleasurable experience and the techniques involved in producing good-quality results are not difficult to learn, many enthusiasts reach a point of frustration when, having acquired the equipment and the ability to take good pictures, they do not know how to apply it.

The projects, techniques, and subject ideas outlined are designed to provide a constant source of motivation to get out your camera and start shooting whenever you have a spare moment – on holiday, for a few hours on a winter's evening, or at a weekend around your home. It is not simply a list of specific things to photograph; each topic aims to stimulate your own ideas and to suggest how to apply familiar techniques in different ways, and how to combine subjects, techniques, and creative approach to produce an almost limitless variety of possibilities.

Camera Techniques

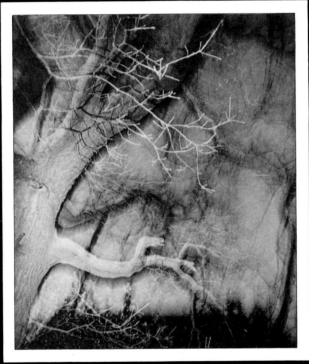

Focusing effects

In a large proportion of the pictures taken by amateur photographers the whole of the image is recorded with equal sharpness. A camera with a standard lens focused at, say, 16 feet (5 metres) and stopped down to f8 or f11 will record in sharp focus everything from a short distance in front of the camera to infinity. The ability to use those aspects of an image which are out of focus in a controlled way is, however, a powerful creative tool and can be exploited to great effect in both composition and mood.

Depth of field is the area before and beyond the point of focus which is recorded with acceptable sharpness and it is dependent on a number of factors: depth of field reduces as the point of focus becomes closer to the camera, it is more shallow with long-focus lenses and at wide apertures, and it increases as the point of focus moves away from the camera and as the aperture of the lens is made smaller. The most marked difference between the 'in-focus' and 'out-of-focus' areas will be produced therefore when a long-focus lens is used at a wide aperture and focused at a point quite close to the camera.

The most basic use of out-of-focus areas in an image is to create a smooth, unobtrusive tone from background details to provide good contrast and separation from the main subject of a picture, such as a portrait for instance. Where you have bold tonal or colour

contrasts in the background area you can create quite exciting swirls of colour and tone by keeping them well out of focus; highlights will record as large, luminous discs.

It can be equally interesting to use an out-of-focus foreground such as foliage to create a soft screen of colour or tone between the camera and the subject. There are also occasions when it can be effective to focus on a foreground detail and allow the subject or distant scene to be out of focus, and it is also possible to produce striking abstractions by shooting with the entire image out of focus.

An SLR or view camera is essential for this type of picture since they enable the out-of-focus effects to be assessed visually, whereas with a viewfinder camera the image is shown completely sharp regardless of the point where the lens is focused.

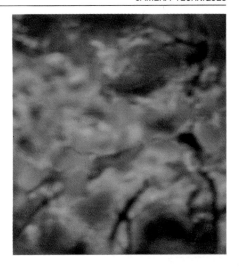

Left An out-of-focus foreground can be an effective way of composing a picture as well as creating an impression of depth. A wide aperture and a long-focus lens have aided the effect. Nikon F; 200 mm lens; 1/500 at f4; Ektachrome 64.

Above right The lens has been focused between the branch and a more distant tree; although the picture is unsharp, there is an 'edge' effect where the two planes meet. Nikon F2; 105 mm lens; 1/250 at f2.8; Ektachrome 64.

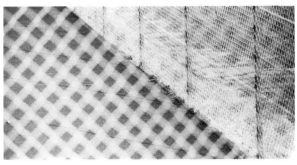

Right Shooting through an out-of-focus wire-mesh fence has created a texture screen effect and a degree of abstraction. Nikon F3; 150 mm lens; 1/250 at f5.6; Ilford FP4.

Below right The slightly surreal image of this breakwater has been produced by focusing on the close group of pebbles and using a wide aperture to give a very shallow depth of field. Rolleicord; 1/250 at f4; Ilford FP4.

Using mirrors

There are a number of ways in which mirrors can be exploited to add interest and impact to a photograph, and they can also be used to create abstract images. A large piece of plate-glass mirror can be used as a surface for a still-life shot where the reflected image of the subject can form an additional element of composition and also provide an interesting foreground by reflecting the tones and colours created on the background. A more interesting effect can be produced by using thin, flexible plastic sheets which can be obtained from art supply stores and paper suppliers; the sheets are highly reflective when smooth, but they can be rippled like the surface of water to produce a similar distortion of the subject.

A small pocket mirror can be employed to create double images by holding it close to the lens and almost parallel to the lens axis. By moving it up and down slightly across the lens it is possible to get an inverted repeat image of a distant subject and also to superimpose an object from outside the direct view of the lens on to the image on which it is focused. A conventional mirror can also be used in the background of a picture and angled to the sun so that it creates a 'star-burst' of light in the background. Used in a similar way but outside the picture area, a mirror can provide an effective second source of light when shooting in daylight either outdoors or indoors.

It is possible to buy good-quality mirror surfaces on flexible plastic bases which can be easily cut, rolled, or crinkled. These can be used to produce abstract and distorted images of a subject by placing the mirror close to the lens and focusing on the subject's reflection. Another possibility is to make a cylinder out of a flexible mirror, with the surface on the inside; if you place this over the camera lens and shoot through it, this will produce a sharp central image of the subject which is surrounded by a circular frame of abstract streaks of colour and tone.

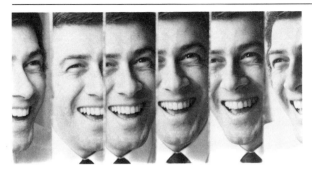

Left Small strips of mirror glass were taped together to form a continuous but uneven surface to provide this repeated reflection of a face. The effect is given added incongruity by the fact that each image is seen from a slightly different viewpoint. Hasselblad; 150 mm lens; f11 with studio flash; Ilford FP4.

Left Added impact has been given to this simple still life of seashell by placing it on a sheet of flexible mirrored plastic which was then curved to produce the distorted reflection. Pentax 6 × 7; 150 mm lens; f16 with studio flash; Ilford FP4.

Left These two pictures were made by using a small mirror held in front of the camera lens in the manner shown in the illustrations (right). By moving the position and angle of the mirrors it is possible to alter the juxtaposition of the images. The use of a front-silvered mirror prevents the formation of ghosting on the reflection. Rollei SLX; 150 mm lens; f11 with studio flash; Ilford FP4.

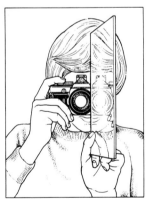

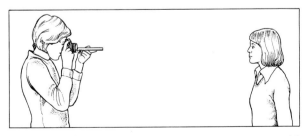

Using coloured lights

In most cases when artificial lighting is used for photography the aim is to match carefully the colour temperature of the source to the colour balance of the film but many interesting effects can be produced by placing coloured acetates over the lights to produce a colour bias. One useful technique is to use a filtered lamp to illuminate a white background to give a colour effect. This is quite different from the effect of a coloured paper background, and if you use two or more lights with different-coloured filters a wide range of effects is possible. It can also be effective to use a light with a filter of the same colour as the background to create a purer, more intense colour.

Using coloured lights to illuminate the subject can produce interesting effects. With a portrait, for instance, a colour filter can be added to a back light or rim light to create a coloured halo of light around the model's hair. It is important to realize that the effect tends to be greater on the film than appears visually and this can look gimmicky if it is overdone. Where a more abstract effect is required, several different-coloured light sources can be used to illuminate a subject; in addition to the effects created in the illuminated areas there will also be interesting colour variations in the shadows.

By carefully balancing the light from two or more sources it is possible to produce a normal colour balance in some areas of the subject with a colour bias in others. For example, if one light was fitted with a red filter and another with a cyan filter of the same strength, a normal colour balance would be produced where the lights were mixed equally, but areas of shadow would produce a variety of colours.

A further variation is to use a colour filter over the camera lens as well as over the lights. You could illuminate the main part of the subject with a small spot of filtered light and use a filter of the complementary colour over the camera lens. This would produce a normal colour balance in the central part of the image but the remainder of the picture would have a colour bias equal to that of the filter on the camera.

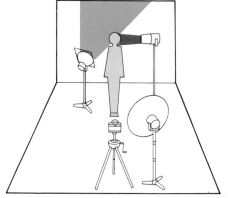

Above A blue filter was placed over the light which was used to illuminate the blue paper background to give it added saturation, and a red filter was placed over the hair light. The model's face was lit with unfiltered light. (See diagram, above right.) Rollei SLX; 150 mm lens; f8 with studio flash; Ektachrome 64.

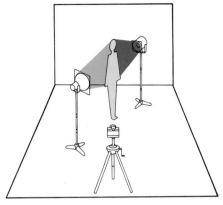

Above A very theatrical effect has been created in this shot by using two rim lights only, one fitted with a blue filter and the other with an orange filter. (See diagram, above right.) Rollei SLX; 150 mm lens; f8 with studio flash; Ektachrome 64.

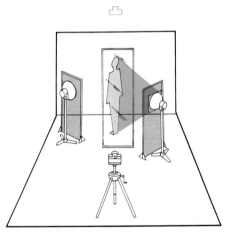

Above A blue acetate filter was placed over the light which illuminated the sheet of water-spattered glass which is acting as a texture screen in this nude shot. A Wratten 81C filter was used on the camera lens to add warmth to the skin tones of the model. (See diagram, above right.) Pentax 6 × 7; 150 mm lens; f11 with studio flash; Ektachrome 64.

Flash effects

Most photographers use flash either as a sole means of illumination indoors or occasionally as a means of balancing lighting contrast when shooting outdoors in sunlight. A portable flash unit can, however, be used most effectively as a means of creating unusual and dramatic effects. The simplest method is to use the flash to illuminate the foreground subject and alter the balance between it and the background; in this way it is possible, for instance, to create the impression of a dusk or night-time shot in broad daylight.

The procedure is to select the correct aperture for the flash-to-subject distance and then to set the shutter speed 2 or 3 stops faster than that indicated by the exposure meter. This will produce a normally exposed foreground but an under-exposed background. This can be more easily done with a camera that has a between-the-lens shutter as opposed to a focal plane shutter because the flash will synchronize up to 1/500 sec rather than 1/60 sec or 1/125 sec which is the limit with a focal plane shutter. The technique is quite possible, however, with

the focal plane shutter but you will be more restricted in your choice of aperture and flash-to-subject distance.

The technique is particularly useful when shooting colour pictures because in addition to altering the lighting balance you can also alter the colour balance of the foreground and background. If you were shooting a portrait and you placed a red filter over the flash you would have a picture with a normal background but the model would have a red colour cast. If you were then to place the red filter over the camera lens and put a cyan filter of the same strength over the flash the result would be a picture with a red cast over the background but with the model recorded with normal colour balance.

Movement is another interesting possibility which can be exploited. If a fairly slow shutter speed is selected, say $\frac{1}{4}$ or $\frac{1}{2}$ sec, and either the subject or the camera allowed to move during the exposure, the result will be an image where part of the scene is recorded as a blur but the part illuminated predominantly by the flash is recorded sharply.

Above A blue filter was used over the camera lens and a red filter over the flash to produce the bold contrast between the sky and the telephone box. Nikon F2; 24 mm lens; 1/125 at f8; Ektachrome 64.

Left The camera was vibrated during a slow exposure to produce this effect of part sharp and part blurred image. Nikon F3: 1/4 at f16: Ektachrome 64.

Far left The dusk effect of this shot was created by using the correct aperture for the flash exposure but setting the shutter speed 3 stops faster than that indicated by the exposure meter. Rollei SLX; 50 mm lens; 1/250 at f11; Ektachrome 64.

15

Projector effects

A slide projector can be used in a variety of ways to produce interesting and unusual effects, either by projecting a slide on to the subject or by projecting a slide of the subject on to an object or a surface. This must obviously be done in a situation where you can restrict and control the ambient light. Ideally you need a room which can be made dark and one or two studio lights which can be fitted with snoots to limit the spill of light, since although it is often necessary to light the subject in addition to the illumination provided by the projector, too much light will make the image weak and indistinct. If you wished to project a slide on to a person's face or body, more interest and form could be created by using small spots of light to pick out some of the outlines of the subject (by rim lighting, for example), but as this lighting will in effect erase the projected image it is important to prevent it from spilling on to areas where you want this to predominate.

The angle of the projection in relation to the subject will also affect its form. If, for in-stance, the projector is used from close to the camera position the image will be quite flat, but if it is used from an angle of, say, 45° it will create shadows within the subject. The background will help to control the effect of the picture; if you position your subject against a black background its outline will be clearly defined by the projected image, but if the subject is placed against a white background image will be continued on to it, and the shape of the subject will be less distinct.

An alternative method is to project your subject either on to a surface to create a textured effect or on to an object to create a multiple image – in this way a face could be combined with, say, an apple. This would also have to be lit very selectively so that its shape and form were revealed without degrading the projected image. When shooting in colour it is important to use tungsten light film to achieve correct balance for the projected image; if you wished to light your subject with flash you could use a daylight-to-tungsten conversion filter over the projector lens.

Right This abstract nude was produced by projecting a transparency of a physiogram on to her body, as shown in the diagram (below right). Rim lighting was used to establish her outline and some modelling but was tightly controlled with snoots to prevent the light spilling on to the projected image and degrading it. Rollei SLX; 150 mm lens; 1/2 at f8; Ektachrome tungsten film.

Opposite A piece of white card was positioned close to the model's head so that the projected image of a lake scene continued on to the background. The projector was placed close to the camera and no other lighting was used. The set-up is shown in the diagram (below left). Pentax 6 × 7; 150 mm lens; 1/2 at f11; Ektachrome tungsten film.

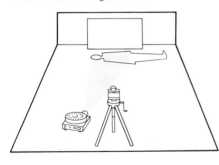

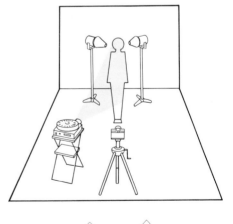

Polarized light

A polarizing filter is one of the most useful accessories for general photography since it enables the light from reflective surfaces to be reduced, thereby cutting out unwanted reflections and adding depth and colour. There is another way, however, in which polarizing filters can be used indoors with certain subjects to give unusual and colourful effects. Certain materials – plastics in particular – refract polarized light in a way that creates a wide range of colours in an otherwise colourless object. You will need two polarizing filters for this technique – one on the camera lens and one behind the subject. Since the filter behind the subject is likely to be larger than a conventional polarizing filter you will have to obtain a polarizer in the form of a plastic sheet (available from most scientific and optical suppliers).

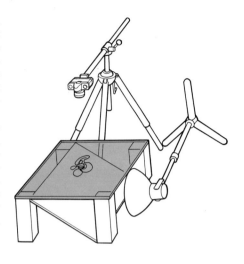

As the effect depends on refraction the object to be photographed is best lit from behind. A simple method is to make a small wooden frame, the same size as your polarizing sheet, and to attach the sheet to one side of the frame with a piece of tracing paper fixed to the other side. With your subject positioned in front of the screen and a studio light, such as a photoflood, directed at it from behind, you will have a 'polarized light box'. The colour effect can be controlled by rotating the polarizer on the camera in the normal way. The nature of the object will, however, determine the success of the technique, and as the colour refraction is dependent largely on the stresses created in the manufacture it

Left The polarized crystals in the picture on the right were photographed using the arrangement shown in this diagram.

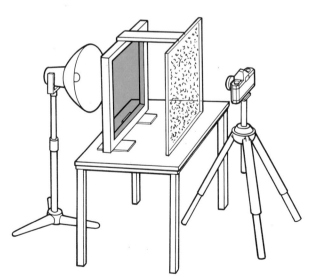

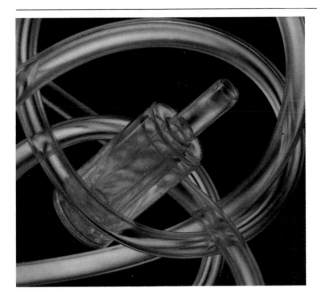

Far left This set-up was used to produce the still-life arrangement of plastic tubes in the picture on the left.

Left This unusual image was produced by arranging a length of plastic tubing and a fermentation lock of the sort used in wine-making on the light box shown in the illustration (far left). Pentax 6 × 7; 150 mm lens; f16 with studio flash; Ektachrome 200.

will be necessary to experiment with a variety of items. Moulded plastics such as jugs, bottles, boxes, and even plastic bags or tape will produce these effects, and they can be further emphasized by using two or more layers. Glass unfortunately will not work.

If you have close-up equipment such as a bellows unit or a macro lens you will be able to produce dramatic effects from crystals. Hypo is ideal, and a good method is to make a saturated solution of hypo, pour it on to a sheet of clean glass and allow it to evaporate. The result will be a crystalline screen which can be placed in front of the polarized light box and photographed in the way described.

Left Hypo crystals which had formed on a sheet of glass by evaporation were the basis of this picture; extension tubes were needed to obtain sufficient magnification. Nikon F3; 50 mm lens with extension tubes; f16 with studio flash; Ektachrome 200.

Strobe effects

Strobe lighting, which is common in discotheques, produces a regular pulse of light at controllable intervals. When a strobe light is used in conjunction with a slow shutter speed and a moving subject the effect produced is a series of individual images on the film. The number of images will depend on the duration of the exposure and the flash rate of the strobe; with a setting of 20 flashes per second and a 1/2 sec exposure, for instance, you would get 10 images on the film.

The background should be either black or very dark so that the images can be clearly seen, and to prevent the background density building up with each exposure the lighting should be shielded from the background area. It is important to light the subject so that the static elements are less well lit than the rest since this will also build up in density; rim lighting is therefore often the most effective way of lighting a strobe shot.

If you do not have access to a stroboscopic

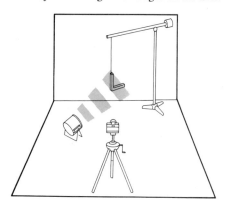

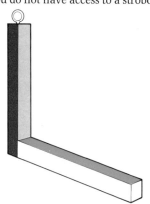

Right This abstract image was produced by suspending an L-shaped piece of wood with brightly painted surfaces and allowing it to swing from side to side and rotate while being illuminated by a stroboscopic light and given an exposure of 2 sec. The equipment and set-up are shown in the illustrations (above). Rollei SLX; 150 mm lens; f5.6; Ektachrome 200.

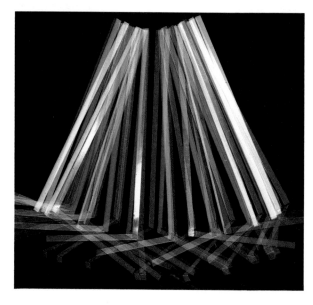

flash it is possible to produce equally effective pictures with certain subjects using ordinary portable flash units. You can do this by asking the model to move in slow motion and setting the camera on time or bulb exposure while the flash is fired manually at the necessary intervals. Providing the room is dark it does not matter if it takes minutes to complete the image; this method has the added advantage that the position of the model can be predetermined for each exposure. With a camera that has a multiple exposure facility it is also possible simply to repeat exposures on the X setting, using the camera shutter for each exposure without advancing the film.

Another possibility is to use more than one light source to create a more clearly defined image, and in some instances it can help to shoot half the sequence with the light in one position and the other half with the light from a different angle. You should use a tripod so that the camera position is identical for each image. It is important to do a number of trial runs to ensure that the action and lighting produce a good separation of images and to help you determine the best intervals at which to make the exposures.

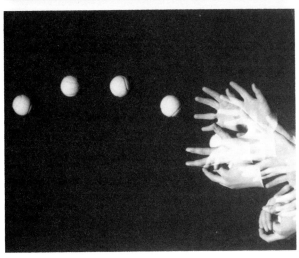

Left These two pictures show the effect that can be created by photographing quite simple movements with the aid of a stroboscopic light and a long exposure in a darkened room. In both cases the image is given clarity by lighting the subject from one side so that the highlights of one exposure are juxtaposed against the shadows of the other. Rollei SLX; 80 mm lens; f8; Kodak Tri-X.

Ultra-violet light

Just as the invisible infra-red radiation can be used to take photographs, so can the ultra-violet rays beyond the opposite end of the spectrum. However, unlike infra-red, ultra-violet light does not require a special film but it does need a special light source. The most convenient form of ultra-violet radiation for photography is the type of lamp known commonly as black light, so-called because it produces a minimal amount of visible light (unlike sun-lamps which are not suitable). Black-light lamps can be obtained from electrical supply stores in the form of either fluorescent tubes or filament bulbs; either is suitable. You will also need an ultra-violet filter such as the Kodak 2A for the camera lens in order to eliminate any risk of reflected radiation since you will be photographing the effect of the ultra-violet light on a fluorescing object and other reflections will

Right This rather surrealistic image was created by dressing the model in garments made from fluorescent fabrics. Since the ultra-violet source was the only lighting used, the model herself has not recorded, leaving the apparently disembodied clothes with their eerie glow. Rollei SLX; 150 mm lens; 1 at f4; Ektachrome 200.

Far right This still-life arrangement was produced by placing the glasses on a sheet of flexible mirror paper which was slightly wrinkled. The multi-coloured effect was created by fixing several sheets of different-coloured fluorescent paper behind and just above the picture area and illuminating them with the ultra-violet light source. A small amount of tungsten light was used to add a little extra detail to the glasses. Rollei SLX; 150 mm lens; 4 at f11; Ektachrome 200.

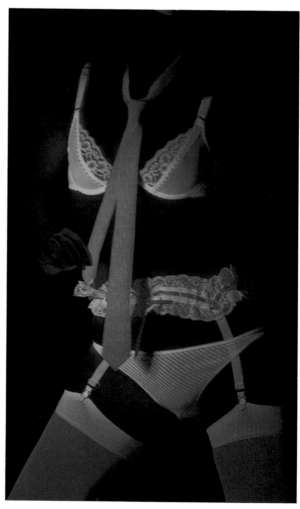

diminish the effect; for this reason the pictures must be taken in a darkened room.

The way that the ultra-violet light works is that certain elements absorb the energy from the ultra-violet radiation and in doing so become 'excited' and release brilliant colours. This is called fluorescence and the effect is used sometimes in discotheques and window displays. The most dramatic results will be achieved with objects that contain a high proportion of these elements, and the easiest way to discover them is to direct your blacklight source at different items to see the reaction. Many everyday objects will react in this way and if you wish to shoot something that is not fluorescent you can coat it with a fluorescent paint or dye which can be obtained from art supply stores and craft shops.

Exposures will be quite long, so a fast film can be an advantage; either daylight or tungsten light film is suitable. With an average fluorescent subject and the ultra-violet light about 2 feet ($\frac{1}{2}$ metre) away the exposure on an ISO 200/24° film will be about 1 sec at f5.6 or f8. It is advisable to make a test exposure or to bracket your exposures.

Painting with light

In most pictures where artificial lighting is used, the light source remains fixed for the duration of the exposure once it has been positioned. During a time exposure, however, it can be effective to move a light source during the exposure. This is a particularly useful technique when photographing a large interior in which the available light is unsatisfactory. It can be done with flash or a continuous light such as a photoflood lamp, although the latter is likely to give a more even and shadow-free effect. The camera should be placed on a tripod and an aperture selected which enables an exposure of a minute or so to be given without the available light registering too strongly. The shutter must now be opened on a time setting. With a photoflood you can now simply swing the lamp in wide sweeps across the picture area, moving it from side to side and top to bottom. It will also help to produce a more even, shadow-free effect if you move your position from one side of the camera to the other during the exposure.

Left An assistant traced the outline of the girl with two flashlights (one with a red filter) taped together in a darkened room with the shutter held open. The flash was then fired to illuminate the girl. Rollei SLX; 150 mm lens; 15 (approx.) at f11 with studio flash; Ektachrome 200.

Above This interior shot used a long exposure with the camera mounted on a tripod; a single light source was moved across the field of view during the exposure. Nikon F; 24 mm lens; 30 at f16; Ilford FP4.

Right In this night shot the subject was illuminated with six flashes with the tripod-mounted camera set on a time exposure. Each flash was fired from a different position; filters were used over the flash for three exposures. Rollei SLX; 80 mm lens; f8; Ektachrome 200.

Exposure must be largely by trial and error although an exposure reading taken from one illuminated section can be used as a basis for a test. If, for instance, 5 sec at f22 is given with the lamp illuminating about one-tenth of the picture area, an exposure of 50 sec could be tried as a test. A flash unit can be used in a similar way by aiming it at a different section each time and flashing it manually.

It can also be interesting to try illuminating exterior scenes at night or dusk in a similar way. Unusual effects can be created by firing a flash from 10 or 12 different positions and in different directions in a woodland scene, for instance, and when shooting in colour you could use colour filters over the flash unit for some of the flashes. Another interesting variation on the moving-light technique is to let a model trace a pattern of light with a flashlight in a darkened studio with the camera on a time setting. Make a flash exposure in the normal way to illuminate the model when the pattern is complete.

False colour effects

With the majority of colour photographs the intention of the photographer is to reproduce the colours of the scene as faithfully as the characteristics of the film will allow. Obviously there are small adjustments which are frequently made, for example the use of a Wratten 81A filter to add a little warmth to a 'cool' scene, but there is considerable potential in the use of techniques which *completely* alter the colour quality of a scene to produce pictures with quite unusual and dramatic qualities. One of the more extreme measures is to shoot with one of the quite strong orange or yellow filters which are intended for use with black and white film.

Above This picture of a bubble-gum dispenser shows the effect of processing transparency film in colour negative chemicals. Rollei SLX; 150 mm lens; 1/60 at f8; Ektachrome 64; C41 process.

Left The blue cast of this dusk shot has been emphasized by shooting on a tungsten light film. Nikon F3; 105 mm lens; 1/8 at f11; Ektachrome 160 tungsten film.

This technique is most effective with subjects that are fairly monochromatic or have a high contrast range such as a silhouette or a back-lit subject.

A rather more subtle approach is to use the colour correction filters which are available as gelatin squares in a variety of strengths and colours. These can simply be taped on to the front of the lens or, preferably, used in a special holder. They are not expensive and although rather vulnerable to damage can be used many times if handled carefully. A selection of about six filters – cyan, magenta, yellow, blue, red, and green – in strength 10 will give you a variety of possible combinations and effects. The most obvious way to use them is to introduce a colour cast into a scene but equally effective and often more intriguing is to use them to exaggerate an existing colour cast or colour quality in a subject: a red filter, for instance, would add depth and intensity to a still-life shot of red roses, or a blue filter could be used to exaggerate the bluish quality of an overcast day, in fact changing what could be a fault into a positive and dramatic quality.

The film itself can be employed to produce 'false' colour by shooting artificial light film in daylight, for instance, and vice versa. A less obvious method is to shoot on colour transparency film but to have it processed in colour negative chemicals; this results in an image where both tones and colours are reversed and is most effective with subjects that have a bold and contrasting colour and tonal range.

Left In this shot taken in open shade the bluish quality is heightened by the use of a Kodak CC 20 cyan gelatin filter. Nikon F3; 105 mm lens; 1/60 at f8; Ektachrome 64.

Below Here, the rich colour was produced by means of an orange filter of the type normally used for black and white photography. Nikon F3; 24 mm lens; 1/60 at f8; Ektachrome 64; orange filter.

Glass montage

There are a number of methods of combining two separate images on to one piece of film, for example making a double exposure. The glass montage technique, however, has the advantage that you are able to view the result quite accurately before the exposure is made, but it does need to be done in subdued light and requires lighting equipment. The underlying principle is that if a piece of good-quality glass is placed in front of the camera lens at an angle of 45° to the optical axis the camera will 'see through' it to the subject at which it is aimed, while at the same time another subject which is positioned at right angles to the optical axis and suitably illuminated will be reflected into the camera and will combine with the first image.

As with a double exposure the images will only be clear where the light tones of one image are juxtaposed against the darker tones of the other but this can be controlled by the lighting arrangement of each subject, which of course must be done quite independently in each case. This technique is obviously only suitable for quite static subjects

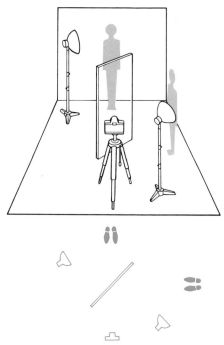

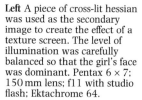

Left A piece of cross-lit hessian was used as the secondary image to create the effect of a texture screen. The level of illumination was carefully balanced so that the girl's face was dominant. Pentax 6 × 7; 150 mm lens; f11 with studio flash; Ektachrome 64.

Right This rather sinister image was produced by lighting the face so that one side was in deep shadow. Pentax 6 × 7; 150 mm lens; f16 with studio flash; Ektachrome 64.

Above The diagram shows a typical set-up: the main subject is in front of the camera and the secondary subject at right angles to it.

such as a portrait or a still life, and a further restriction is that both subjects must be at a similar distance from the camera to enable both to be focused sharply, but it can nevertheless be put to effective use.

Very convincing 'tricks' can be photographed – combining two faces, for example, one lit on the opposite side to the other and combined in the centre, or making an apple appear to be inside a bottle. This is also an effective means of creating texture effects in portrait or glamour pictures, for example by using a piece of obliquely illuminated fabric as the right-angle image. It is quite simple to use landscape or exterior images in combination with, say, a portrait or a still life by taking a large colour print as the second image. Even a colour trans-

parency could be projected on to a tracing-paper screen placed at the right-angle position in a similar way to the back projection technique described on pages 30–1. In addition to photographic images it is of course also possible to use paintings, drawings, or even lettering as the secondary element of the glass montage.

Special requirement

An SLR or view camera is best although it is possible with other types

A firm tripod

A piece of high-quality glass

A stand and clamp to support the glass

Back projection

This technique enables a colour transparency to be used as a background image for a subject. Although it is possible to use this method with a portrait or a figure shot it is easier and more effective with static subjects such as a still life. It requires a room in which the light can be eliminated, a table for the still life, a camera with a double exposure capability and a firm tripod together with a projector and a tracing-paper screen, and a piece of black fabric (velvet is ideal).

The tracing-paper screen should be placed as close to the still-life arrangement as possible and the projector positioned behind the screen at a distance which enlarges the transparency to fill the screen, or at least cover the background area of the shot. If space is restricted, a good-quality mirror, preferably front silvered, can be used so that the projector can be positioned to the side.

The lighting should be arranged so that the minimum amount spills on to the screen. An exposure reading should be made and then the screen covered with the black fabric, and the first exposure made. The camera must not now be moved! The black fabric is removed from the screen and the projector switched on and the image checked for size

and focus. All other lighting must now be extinguished and an exposure calculation made for the projected image. After resetting the shutter and exposure *without* moving the film, the second exposure can be made.

The success of this technique depends largely on ensuring the correct balance of exposure and lighting between the still-life foreground and the projected background and also in arranging a convincing join between the base of the screen and the surface of the still-life bench (this can usually be masked or obscured by objects in the still-life arrangement). It is the need to make two separate exposures that restricts the technique to static subjects although it can be done with one exposure for a portrait shot.

The restrictions and limitations are considerable, however: the subject lighting must be reduced to avoid degrading the projected image, the screen must be positioned much further behind the subject to avoid light spill, and the projected image will be of a much lower intensity than with conventional studio lighting. This is why professional photographers use the far more expensive and complex front projection system for non-static subjects such as fashion photography.

Right The diagram shows the set-up with projector, tracing-paper screen, still-life arrangement, and camera.

This series of three pictures shows the individual stages of the back projection. **(Opposite left)** The foreground is lit in the normal way and the tracing-paper screen has been removed from the window-frame. **(Opposite right)** The slide of the flames was projected in darkness on to the screen pinned on the window-frame. **(Below)** This shows the effect of the two exposures combined on one sheet of film. 5 × 4 Arca Swiss camera; 210 mm Symmar lens; Ektachrome tungsten film.

Special requirements

A darkened room

A camera with a double exposure capability

A firm tripod

A slide projector

Lighting equipment

A tracing-paper screen

A piece of black fabric the size of the screen

A table or bench

Tri-colour photographs

When you take a photograph on colour film the image is recorded instantaneously on three separate layers in the emulsion, each sensitive to a different colour of light – red, green, and blue. If, however, you were to make three separate exposures on to the same piece of film, each one through a different filter coloured red, green, or blue, the result would be identical – *providing* nothing had moved between the exposures. This gives rise to a variety of interesting and exciting possibilities. Take, for example, a landscape picture in which nothing at all moved between the exposures except the clouds in the sky. The result would be a perfectly normal picture apart from the clouds which would record as multi-coloured shapes in an otherwise normal blue sky.

The technique is quite simple but requires a camera with a double exposure capability, a firm tripod, and a set of Tri-colour separation filters (available from Kodak). First frame and focus your camera and lock it firmly into position, then take an exposure reading in the normal way and make an exposure through the red filter at the indicated setting. Reset the shutter *without* winding the film, and make exposures through the green and blue filters (these require an increase in exposure). With daylight film under normal conditions 1½ stops extra for the green and 2 extra for the blue filter will give a normal rendering of the static elements of the subject.

Having established the technique you will be surprised at the variety of ways in which it can be exploited, the most obvious being with a static scene which contains some moving elements, such as a street scene with cars or people, or a river with rippling water. There are many other ways in which the effect can be created: shifting the point of focus between exposures, for example, or changing the aperture so that background details become more out of focus.

Using a zoom lens to change the image size slightly for each exposure is another way of exploiting the technique and with studio pictures such as a still life you can alter the

lighting angle between exposures so that the distribution of highlight and shadow changes with each colour. Images with bold contrasts and strong highlights will produce very colourful rainbow-like effects and softer pictures will have a more subtle result, but the possibilities and variations which can be created are almost limitless.

Special requirements
A firm tripod
A camera with a double exposure capability
A set of Tri-colour separation filters

Left A lapse of about a minute was allowed between each exposure to enable the clouds to move and produce this effect. Nikon F3; 20 mm lens; 1/125 at f8; Ektachrome 64; red filter exposure.

Right The quite subtle effect of the colour grouping is a result of a low-contrast image and a lack of bold highlights. Nikon F3; 150 mm lens; 1/15 at f16; Ektachrome 64; red filter exposure.

Below Bright highlights and vigorous movement of the water and the branches have produced this dramatic effect. Nikon F3; 105 mm lens; 1/60 at f11; Ektachrome 64; red filter exposure.

Using grain effects

Although the majority of photographs are intended to be sharp, clear, and quite faithful records of a scene there are often occasions where the prime concern is to create a mood or to produce an image with a more interpretative than factual rendering of a subject. This often involves producing pictures where clarity and definition are deliberately sacrificed; soft focus techniques are a good example. Another extremely effective and striking technique is to exploit the grain structure of the film so that individual clumps of black silver in the emulsion become a visible and dominant element of the image. Since the grain structure of an emulsion becomes coarser in relation to its sensitivity it follows that a grainy image will be more easily achieved with a fast film, and this can be further emphasized by push-processing techniques. In

black and white pictures an ISO 400/27° film such as Tri-X can be uprated to ISO 1600/33° by the use of specially formulated developers or increased processing times. There is also an extremely fast film called Kodak 2475 recording film which has a particularly pleasing grain structure that can be rated at up to ISO 3200/36°.

Both over-exposure and over-development will help to produce an enlarged grain structure, and with fairly low-contrast subjects this can also be used to good effect. Since the ultimate effect of the grainy image will depend on the degree of enlargement of the negative it is also an advantage to compose your pictures so that only a small portion of the negative is needed. When making prints it is vital that the image should be perfectly sharp right into the corners of the picture

since the effectiveness of the grainy image will be totally destroyed if the print is even slightly unsharp. With dense negatives and high degrees of enlargement a focusing magnifier is an invaluable aid as it enables you to focus on the actual grains in the negative emulsion. A hard grade of paper will also emphasize the granularity of the image.

The same principles apply when shooting in colour, the major difference being that it is under-exposure rather than over-exposure that will emphasize the grain structure of a colour transparency, but a fast film, push-processing, and a high degree of enlargement are also key factors. As a rule, grain is more noticeable with subjects that have areas of even tone and lack bold contrasts and a lot of detail. A useful trick is to use a fog or pastel filter on the camera when shooting to keep the image contrast low, leaving you scope to increase it and emphasize the grain at the processing and printing stages.

Far left A very small section of a 35 mm negative was enlarged on to a hard paper to produce this grainy landscape. Nikon F3; 75 mm lens; 1/250 at f8; Kodak Tri-X.

Above This portrait was shot with Kodak 2475 recording film which was uprated to ISO 3200/36° to increase the grain further. Soft lighting was used so that the print could be made on a hard grade of paper. Nikon F3; 150 mm lens; f22 with studio flash; Kodak 2475 recording film.

Left The grain in this picture of an old lady was created by making a contrasty negative from a colour transparency shot on a fast film and then enlarging a small section of the image to emphasize the grain. Nikon F3; 105 mm lens; 1/125 at f8; Ektachrome EL ISO 400/27°.

Double exposure

Of all the ways of producing a multiple image in the camera a double exposure is probably the least complicated. The technique does require some care, however, and the images must be well planned to avoid disappointing results. If your camera does not have a device that permits double exposures to be made it is possible to mark the starting position of the film relative to the film track when the camera is loaded and then rewind for the second shot – this must be done very carefully.

There are two important pitfalls to avoid

when making a double exposure, one is over-exposure and the other is badly juxtaposed images. When calculating the exposure it is necessary to reduce each exposure by half when a fairly simple juxtaposition of two normal-toned images is being made. It is also vital to compose each picture so that the key features of each image are not lost when the two are combined. It is easiest to think of the film as being 'used up' whenever highlights or light-toned areas are recorded, and any subsequent light areas superimposed on the

Right This double exposure of a studio-lit nude and a seascape was made in a slide duplicator; the same effect could have been made without this piece of equipment, but with far more trouble and less control. (Nude) Nikon F3; 105 mm lens; f11 with studio flash; Ektachrome 64. (Seascape) Nikon F3; 400 mm lens; 1/125 at f8; Ektachrome 200.

same part of the picture on the second exposure will have little or no effect.

The essence of a well-planned double exposure is to ensure that the important light tones of one exposure are superimposed on a dark tone or shadow of the other where the film has only been partially 'used up'. In practice it is often preferable to allow one of the images to predominate; this can largely be controlled by the relative exposures, by reducing the exposure of the 'background' image to a quarter or even an eighth (or 2 or 3 stops) of that calculated while reducing the exposure of the dominant image only slightly, by perhaps $\frac{1}{2}$ stop.

Other ways in which one image can be subdued in favour of the other is to shoot the background image out of focus, or to use a colour filter to create a colour cast: for example, the primary image could be given slightly less than a normal exposure with a reddish filter and the secondary image could be given 2 stops less with a bluish filter.

Where a quite complicated superimposition is planned and you have a camera with a ground glass screen or can remove the pentaprism from an SLR camera, it is a good idea to trace the main outline of your first image on to a piece of tracing paper or clear film to help you compose the second image.

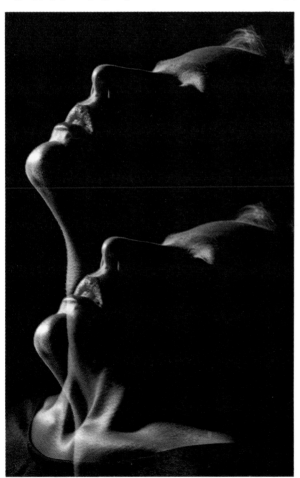

Left Shooting multiple exposures against a black background, as in this example, means that you do not have to decrease the individual exposures and it is easier to plan and visualize the finished effect. Nikon F3; 150 mm lens; f11 with studio flash; Ektachrome 64.

Infra-red film

Infra-red film can be purchased in cartridges with 20 exposures in 35 mm format in both colour and black and white. It is designed primarily for aerial survey work but it can be used to great effect by photographers who like to experiment with the image and colour quality of their pictures. The results of using the colour version of the film are a little difficult to predict since it records the infra-red light which is reflected by the subject and this is of course invisible. Infra-red colour film is intended for use with a yellow filter, a Wratten 12, but it is possible to vary the effects by experimenting with alternatives.

Exposure cannot be calculated in the normal way as metering systems are of course based on visible light, but with the Wratten 12 filter in normal daylight conditions ISO 100/21° will be found to be a good starting point; it is advisable to bracket exposures at least $\frac{1}{2}$ stop each side, however, and preferably 1 stop each side. As a general rule it is better to err on the side of under-exposure as this will emphasize the colour differences. In addition to its strange colour response infra-red colour film increases the contrast and

Above This black and white shot was taken with Kodak infra-red film using a deep red filter. The exposure was calculated in the normal way, rating the film at ISO 100/21, and was bracketed 1 stop each side. The densest negative proved to be the best. Nikon F3; 150 mm lens; 1/60 at f8.

allowance should be made when framing the image to avoid extremes in subject contrast and lighting.

Black and white infra-red film also offers interesting pictorial possibilities and will produce images where green vegetation, for example, is reproduced as near white. Pictures taken on this film often have a rather strange, glowing quality, particularly effective in landscape photography, where its ability to reduce the effects of haze are an advantage. For black and white pictures a deep red filter can be used to record the infra-red reflectance as well as the visible red light, but for a true infra-red effect the visually opaque Wratten 87 filter must be used, with

exposure calculation made by trial and error. Unlike the colour version, black and white infra-red film can produce negatives with insufficient contrast and it is wise to experiment with exposure and development times for the best effect.

Great care should be taken when loading and unloading infra-red film as it is very vulnerable to fogging, and ideally this should be carried out in darkness or in very deep shadow. It is also possible to use a portable flash unit as a light source for infra-red photography; with the Wratten 87 filter taped in front of the tube the flash will not be visible to the eye, but again the exposure must be established by a series of tests.

Left These two pictures show the effect of Kodak infra-red colour transparency film: (above) taken with a sepia Cokin filter, (below) taken without a filter. The results are somewhat unpredictable and it is wise to experiment with both different filtration and different exposures. A good starting point is to rate the film at ISO 100/21 with a Wratten 12 filter. Nikon F3; 35 mm lens; 1/125 at f8.

Using blur

One of the more intriguing aspects of the photographic process is the effect of blur which occurs when the image moves on the film during the exposure. Like many things in photography, when this occurs accidentally it invariably creates an unpleasant effect and produces disappointing pictures. However, used in a careful and controlled way, the effects of blur can be used to create both exciting and beautiful images.

The duration of the exposure is the key factor and to a degree it is a question of trial and error since the effects of a moving image are difficult to predict. As with exposure effects you should experiment by 'bracketing' shutter speeds as the effect of blur at an exposure of, say, 1/2 sec can be radically different from that at 1/8 sec.

The most basic technique is to photograph a moving subject at a slow shutter speed with the camera mounted on a tripod. Running water in a river is a good example to take as although the static elements of the scene such as rocks and trees will be recorded normally when photographed at an exposure of, say, 1 sec, the water will appear smoke-like with wisps of tone. Other subjects which can be treated in this way are people or traffic in a street scene, or wind-blown foliage in a woodland scene.

A common problem is that the slower shutter speeds cannot be used because the light is too bright or the film is too fast even when the smallest aperture is used; in this case neutral density filters, which are available in a variety of strengths, can be used to

Right The swirling effect of the water in this picture has been produced by an exposure of several seconds with the camera mounted on a tripod. A polarizing filter and small aperture were used to make this possible. Nikon F3; 20 mm lens; 4 at f16; Kodachrome 25.

reduce the exposure by 1, 2, or 3 stops and so on as required without affecting the colour of the image.

More complex effects can be produced by shooting a moving subject with a hand-held camera. By 'panning' the camera with the subject and using a slow shutter speed some parts of the subject will be recorded sharply and others blurred while the static elements of the subject, such as the background, will also be blurred. This technique is very effective with sports and action subjects.

Another method of combining both blur and sharpness within one image is by 'controlled camera shake' which involves shaking the camera in a rhythmical way and simultaneously releasing the shutter. A zoom lens can also be used to create blur by zooming from one end of its range to the other during the exposure.

Above A swiftly moving subject, a slow shutter speed, and a panned camera have all contributed to the effect of this action shot. Nikon F3; 200 mm lens; 1/15 at f22; Ektachrome 64.

Left The almost abstract effect of this woodland shot was created by rotating the camera on its axis during the exposure. A slow shutter speed was used and the camera was mounted on a tripod so that the movement could be controlled more easily. Nikon F2; 28 mm lens; 1/4 at f16; Kodachrome 25.

Freezing movement

The ability of a camera to freeze the action of a moving subject and so reveal details that are not visible to the naked eye has always been one of the most fascinating aspects of the medium. As early as 1872 Edweard Muybridge took a series of pictures of a running horse to prove that at one point all four of its feet were off the ground simultaneously.

Modern camera equipment makes this type of picture relatively straightforward; most cameras except the simplest now have shutter speeds of 1/500, 1/1000, or even 1/2000 sec, and such speeds are fast enough to stop the action of very rapid motion, such as a race horse or a sprinter. Even if your camera has a slower minimum shutter speed you can still take pictures of this kind successfully providing you judge the optimum moment to make the exposure. With many moving subjects there is a point at which the speed of the action slows momentarily – a speedway motor-cycle going into a bend, for instance, or a horse at the peak of a jump – and such moments are also often the most dramatic. If you follow the action by panning your camera with the subject and make the exposure at the second this peak is reached it is possible to produce sharp pictures at quite modest shutter speeds.

In addition to fast shutter speeds, electronic flash units can be used to freeze movement. The small portable units used 'on camera' usually have a very brief flash duration, sometimes as short as 1/10 000 sec; the larger units for studio use do not have the same facility, and as a rule the lower output units produce the briefest flashes.

When you are photographing a subject which has continuous movement, such as water, it is a relatively simple matter to judge the moment of exposure but the problems involved in photographing one precise moment, such as an egg being dropped on to a surface, require a little more planning. One solution is to use a pressure plate. This involves replacing the synchronizing plug end of the cable with two thin strips of brass attached to each terminal, held slightly apart by a spring or rocker device. This is then connected to the flash unit and positioned under the surface on to which the object is to be dropped; the impact will fire the flash while the camera shutter is held open on the 'bulb' setting (this must of course be carried out in a darkened room). It is also possible to make devices that will fire the flash from a sound or when an object passes in front of a photo-electric cell.

Left A relatively slow shutter speed and careful panning have recorded the 200 mph Formula 1 car quite sharply but left the background blurred. Nikon F2AS; 200 mm lens; 1/60 at f16; Kodak Tri-X.

Right Effect created by a flash unit positioned behind the model and aimed towards the camera. Nikon F3; 105 mm lens; f11 with studio flash; Ilford FP4.

Below right The moment of impact has been captured by means of the simple device shown in the diagram. Two small flashes were used and the camera shutter held open on the bulb setting until the flash had been fired by the impact. Rollei SLX; 150 mm lens; f11 with portable flash; Ilford FP4.

Below left The contact device is connected to the synchronizing lead of the flash unit. This trigger mechanism is placed under the surface on to which the object is to be dropped.

Exposure effects

The advent of automated cameras has made the problem of determining the correct exposure much less difficult. For the majority of pictures taken by the amateur photographer a center-weighted TTL meter will give a high ratio of acceptable results without the need for a subjective assessment. On the other hand, it does encourage photographers to stop thinking about exposure and to become dependent on the ability of their camera to do it for them. This not only makes them vulnerable to errors but also deprives them of an important creative control over the quality of their images.

Except for pictures taken under laboratory conditions there is no such thing as 'correct'

exposure, only an exposure which reproduces an image the way you saw it or wanted it to be. Many of the stunning colour images you see in books and magazines would not have had the same effect if the photographer had not modified the exposure that his meter had indicated. When shooting black and white or colour negatives an appreciable degree of variation and control can be exercised at the printing stage but with colour transparency film it is the choice of exposure that determines the final quality of the image.

One of the most valuable ways of gaining experience and confidence in this control of your picture is to 'bracket' your exposures, which simply means making additional ex-

posures each side of the one which you have calculated. If, for example, you make nine exposures at ½-stop stages with the calculated setting in the middle you will be able to see the exact effect that a 4-stop variation can have on the particular film you are using. You will find that over-exposure reduces contrast and colour saturation, producing pictures with a more delicate and high-key quality, whèreas under-exposure will increase the contrast of the image and colours will be stronger, producing pictures with richer tones and a more dramatic quality.

By experimenting in this way under different lighting conditions, with different subjects, and with different types of film, you will quickly learn how to produce a particular image quality at will and also be able to control the mood and effect of your pictures.

Left This shot taken into the light was underexposed by 1 stop to emphasize the small but vivid splash of colour. Nikon F3; 400 mm lens; 1/250 at f8; Ektachrome 200.

Top Texture and colour were accentuated by under-exposure of ½ stop, ensuring that the highlights were not bleached out. Rollei SLX; 150 mm lens; 1/125 at f11; Ektachrome 64.
Above The delicate pastel quality was created by over-exposure of 1 stop. Nikon F3; 150 mm lens; 1/60 at f8; Ektachrome 200.

Filters for dramatic black and white

Normal panchromatic black and white films such as Kodak Tri-X or Ilford FP4 are designed to give a quite faithful rendering of the colours in a scene in terms of their tonal values, so that, for example, a red object with the same reflective value as a blue object will record as a similar shade of grey on the film. This means that quite often a colourful and dramatic scene may be recorded as a flat grey image when shot in black and white.

It is possible, however, to alter the balance of tones in a photograph by the use of colour filters. This is because the filter passes light of its own colour quite freely but 'holds back' light from other parts of the spectrum. If you imagine a picture consisting of a green landscape with a blue sky and a red house in the foreground the black and white film would see this as equal tones of mid-grey, but if a red filter were placed over the lens the image would be recorded with a very light grey house and a very dark grey sky and landscape, much more dramatic! With a green filter, however, the picture would have an almost white landscape with a near-black house and a dark grey sky, while with a blue filter the sky would be white and the landscape and house a very dark grey.

The effect is dependent on the strength of the filters: a deep red filter will make a blue sky record as nearly black whereas an orange or yellow filter will have a less pronounced effect. Such filters require an increase of exposure according to their density. This is expressed as a filter factor: a filter with a factor of 2X requires a 1-stop increase in exposure, one of 4X requires 2 stops extra, and so on.

The red to yellow range of filters is probably the most widely used, particularly in landscape work, but a green filter, for example, can help to create a more dramatic range of tones in a landscape by making dense green foliage lighter in tone, and it will also improve the tonal rendition of a sunset shot in black and white. A blue filter will accentuate skin tones in character portraits, producing a rich textural quality, similar to the dramatic effect in early photographs

where film was not sensitive to red light. Pictures which are dependent on a textural quality such as wood or stone, for instance, can often be greatly enhanced by the use of a 'contrast' filter of the appropriate colour and it is well worth spending time experimenting with the effects which are possible.

Left A deep blue filter was used in this portrait to emphasize the texture of the model's skin. An additional exposure of 3 stops was required. Nikon F2; 150 mm lens; f5.6 with studio flash; Ilford FP4.

Below left The rich sky tone in this shot, taken as the sun began to go down, was created by the use of a deep red filter. Nikon F2; 24 mm lens; 1/250 at f5.6; Kodak Tri-X.

Right A green filter produced a bold tonal variation between the different shades of green in this Alpine scene. Nikon F3; 105 mm lens; 1/60 at f8; Ilford FP4.

Below right In this shot of weathered wood, an orange filter was used to help produce the bold tones and emphasize the texture. Nikon F2; 105 mm lens; 1/15 at f11; Ilford FP4.

Time exposures

Many people restrict their picture-taking outdoors to the daylight hours and once the sun has gone down or the light is poor they put their cameras away. In doing so, however, they miss a great many opportunities, not simply of taking photographs but of producing pictures with a slightly different quality. When we talk of the light being 'good' we invariably mean the level of illumination, yet it is the *quality* not the *quantity* of light which is crucial to a good photograph.

There are probably a great many photographers who rarely consider using a setting below, say, 1/30 sec on their shutter speed dial, let alone consider an exposure running into seconds or even minutes, but these techniques can open up a whole new range of possibilities since some of the most

beautiful and dramatic effects of light occur when the brightness level is very low. The basic requirement is a firm tripod and a flexible cable release; if your camera does not have a time exposure setting it is possible to obtain a cable release which has a lock incorporated in it and can be used with the shutter on the 'bulb' setting.

The major technical pitfall to allow for is reciprocity failure; this occurs when long exposures of a second or more make the film less sensitive so that at 1/30 sec the film's normal rating may be ISO 100/21° but at 15 sec only ISO 50/18° and at one minute ISO 25/15°. This can only be accurately assessed by making test exposures and it is worthwhile taking perhaps ten shots at progressively longer exposures on your

favourite film so that in future you will be able to judge the effect accurately. In addition, long exposures usually produce a colour bias and this can also be assessed and the necessary correction filter established by means of test exposures.

As well as enabling you to take pictures in very low levels of illumination time exposures also allow you to use very small apertures which in turn can give pictures with tremendous depth of field. Another technique is to use an exposure of several minutes, so that moving traffic or people do not record on the film when you are shooting a building in a busy street. If the light is too bright even with the lens stopped right down you can use a neutral density filter to lengthen the exposure and time.

Far left This shot of the harbour at Calais, taken before sunrise, required an exposure of 2 seconds on ISO 400/27° film. Nikon F3; 105 mm lens; 2 at f3.5; Ektachrome EL.

Left An exposure of 30 seconds was needed for this moonlit seascape with an increase of $1\frac{1}{2}$ stops over that indicated by the exposure meter to allow for reciprocity failure. Nikon F3; 150 mm lens; 30 at f3.5; Ektachrome rated at ISO 200/24°.

Overleaf This picture taken long after sunset needed an exposure of 2 minutes. The light was quite dark and the wet café tables in the foreground have filled what would have been a black void by reflecting light from the sky. Nikon F3; 24 mm lens; 2 min at f5.6; Ektachrome rated at ISO 200/24°.

49

Subject Idea File

Neighbourhood safari

Many photographers regard wildlife photography as a specialized subject requiring elaborate equipment and exotic locations. It is, however, quite possible to take interesting and successful pictures with far more modest facilities. The observant photographer will find a considerable variety of opportunities to take wildlife pictures even in a garden or a park, and although the subjects may not be rare or even dramatic, this is by no means a necessity for a good photograph. Photographing animals or birds in such situations has the advantage that they are more accustomed to the presence of humans and it is often much easier to approach them closely than would be the case with creatures in the wild. Even so, a long-focus lens is a positive asset, especially when shooting small animals or birds.

The secret of shooting this type of picture is to arrange matters so that your subjects come to you rather than to attempt to stalk them. A little observation will soon establish well-frequented spots apart from the obvious ones such as a bird-table in a garden; a freshly dug border in a park, for instance, will attract birds for feeding, and animals such as squirrels or foxes always have established territories and routes. Once you have found such a location you should set up your camera at a convenient viewpoint (but not too close), preferably concealed behind a natural screen such as a bush. Then you must simply wait patiently until your subject comes within range. Avoid making sudden movements and sounds.

It will help to mount your camera on a tripod and to aim and focus it in the selected spot. When choosing a viewpoint do not forget to consider both the lighting and the background as the aim is to create good separation between the subject and the surroundings and to avoid fussy and distracting details in the background. You should also not overlook the possibilities of small creatures such as butterflies, frogs, snails, as these can also make excellent subjects if you have a close-up attachment for your camera.

Far left It is often possible to approach wildfowl in parks very closely, permitting tightly framed images as in this strong composition. Nikon F3; 150 mm lens; 1/125 at f8; Ilford FP4.

Above This semi-tame squirrel on its way to its regular feeding spot was photographed from a relatively close viewpoint. Nikon F3; 200 mm lens; 1/125 at f5.6; Ilford FP4.

Left This thrush was photographed with a 600 mm mirror lens from a distance of about 16 feet (5 metres). The shallow depth of field has helped to isolate the subject from the background and the mirror lens has created the out-of-focus effects on the highlights. Nikon F3; 600 mm lens; 1/250 at f8; Kodak Tri-X.

City lights

Most of the pictures taken outdoors are shot before the sun goes down – for obvious reasons – but those people who live near a large town or city or who are there on holiday or business have a colourful and exciting subject which they can continue to photograph long after dark. You do not need expensive equipment for this type of photography, providing you have a camera which can be used with a time exposure or 'bulb' setting and a firm tripod. However, this approach will restrict you to fairly static subjects whereas a camera with a fast lens of, say, f2 or f1.4 combined with a fast film of ISO

400/27° will enable you to take hand-held shots in most well-lit city streets.

The major problem with pictures of this sort is high contrast, and a subject which to normal vision may seem quite evenly illuminated will record on the film with large areas of dense shadow and some areas that are burnt out. A good way of judging the contrast level of a subject is to view it through half-closed eyes.

In some situations it is often better to shoot pictures before it is *totally* dark when just a trace of light remains in the sky; this is particularly true of illuminated buildings or wide

Right In this shot of Copenhagen taken before it became totally dark, the shape of the building is quite visible against the sky. The foreground reflection in a street fountain forms an additional element in the composition. Pentax S1A; 55 mm lens; 1/30 at f2.8; Ektachrome 200.

views of a street, for example, where a completely dark sky will lose the outlines and leave just bright pools of light in a dark void. Although the brightness level of illuminated signs, shop windows, and street lights is fairly high immediately around the source it 'falls off' quite rapidly further away from it; in darkness such pictures must be framed quite tightly to avoid excessively large areas of dense shadow.

Exposure should be calculated with a great deal of care as readings which include light sources will invariably result in under-exposure, and unless the light source itself is the subject – an illuminated sign, for instance – you must be very careful to exclude it from the meter's view.

The choice of colour film is not too critical since there is such a wide variation in the colour quality of the light sources – fluorescent lights, for example, will produce an unpleasant green cast even on daylight film and where such lighting predominates a correction filter in the order of CC 20˙– 30 magenta should be used. Although a scene which is lit predominantly with tungsten lighting is best shot on artificial light film, scenes which are illuminated with mixed lighting or neon signs are quite satisfactory when exposed on daylight film. As a general rule the faster colour films such as Ektachrome ISO 400/27° are more tolerant of variations in the colour quality of the lighting than slower films such as Kodachrome.

Above left A fast film which has been uprated and a wide aperture lens enable the use of a hand-held camera in most well-lit city streets. Nikon F3; 50 mm lens; 1/125 at f2; Ektachrome EL rated at ISO 800/30°.

Above right The exposure has been calculated to emphasize the rich colours of the neon lights at the expense of other details in this shot of Las Vegas. Nikon F2; 20 mm lens; 1/15 at f3.5; Kodachrome 64.

Food

As well as being a very pleasant way of taking pictures on days when it is cold, wet, or dark, still-life photography is an excellent means of learning the basic skills of composition, lighting, and camera technique. The idea of using food as the main element of a picture session is that it has a rich variety of shape, texture, and colour, all of which are basic to pictorial composition. What is more, it can be acquired easily and at relatively little expense, and used afterwards.

You do not need much in the way of special equipment; the main requirements are a tripod and a bench of convenient height on which to build the still-life arrangement. You will also need a selection of fabrics or background papers of different tones and colours. Lighting equipment need not be complicated; two photoflood lamps on adjustable stands with a tracing-paper screen and a couple of reflectors made of white card or foam polystyrene will enable you to create a wide variety of lighting effects, and even daylight from a window or skylight can be effective.

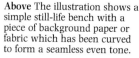

Above The illustration shows a simple still-life bench with a piece of background paper or fabric which has been curved to form a seamless even tone.

Left Fruits and vegetables often have interesting shapes, textures, and patterns which can be revealed by careful framing and lighting to create effective pictures, as this close-up of a cabbage demonstrates. Rollei SLX; 150 mm lens; 1/2 at f16; Ilford FP4.

The best way to start is to assemble a selection of items of varying shapes, sizes, textures, and colours together with a few props. For instance, you may have some eggs, a pineapple, several oranges, a cabbage, a loaf, a basin, a small basket, and an earthenware jug. You will probably have many of these items or will be able to borrow them. Choose a background which can be arranged on the surface of your bench and, if necessary, taped on a wall or a support behind.

The next step is to select the item which you intend to be the focal point of the arrangement and position this on the background, viewing the effect through your tripod-mounted camera. At this stage you can add a second item, experimenting with its position in relation to the first and judging the effect through the viewfinder. Once you are happy with this you can begin to consider if and where other objects are needed to help balance the arrangement. Still-life photography is very much a question of selection, rejection, and juxtaposition combined with sympathetic lighting, with the advantage that unlike many other subjects you have total control over all elements of the image.

Above Two pieces of wood have been used to form a simple setting which adds both interest and atmosphere to this studio still life. Pentax 6 × 7; 150 mm lens; f16 with studio flash; Ilford FP4.

Left This simple arrangement of garlic cloves, onions, and peppers depends on the bold contrast of shapes and tones for its impact. The picture was taken indoors using the light from a window and a white card reflector. Rollei SLX; 150 mm lens; 1/4 at f16; Ilford FP4.

Trees

Most photographers have a favourite subject to which they return again and again: for a glamour photographer it may be a particular model, for a landscape photographer a location which he visits at frequent intervals. One subject which many photographers appear to find particularly appealing is trees. There are a number of reasons for this. Trees have an inherent elegance and nature composes most of them in a pleasing and harmonious way, they come in a wide variety of shapes, sizes, colours, and textures, and they can possess dignity and character. Even more importantly, they are found nearly everywhere except at high altitudes or in extreme climates, and even cities have trees, so that there need never be a shortage of subjects.

The role of a tree in a picture can vary enormously; a small lone tree, for instance, can be the dominant feature of a landscape picture, or a tightly framed image of a gnarled trunk can produce images of an almost abstract quality. Leaves can be used to create pictures ranging from close-ups of delicate colour and texture in spring-time to the broad blaze of rich colour in autumn woodlands. Trees in blossom provide a rich variety of colour and texture, often transforming a landscape for a brief period of time. Even the bare branches of a tree in winter can possess a stark and dramatic beauty, creating images ranging from bold silhouetted shapes against stark skies to delicate traceries covered in frost or snow or veiled in mist.

In numbers, trees can create patterns and perspectives, elements which invariably produce compelling images when used effectively in a composition. This type of picture can be found in both the natural juxtapositions of a forest as well as the organized formality of a tree-lined avenue or a plantation. Trees can quite easily be overlooked as a photographic subject but are in fact a compelling source of pictorial inspiration.

Right Back lighting and the use of a long-focus lens have emphasized the golden foliage and isolated the tree from its surroundings. Nikon F3; 200 mm lens; 1/125 at f8; Kodak Ektachrome 64.

Below right A low viewpoint has silhouetted this elegant tree against an evening sky. A degree of under-exposure has added impact. Nikon F2; 24 mm lens; 1/125 at f8; Kodak Ektachrome 64.

Below left Tight framing and the regularity of the trunks have created a pleasing pattern. The soft lighting has prevented the image becoming too confused and emphasized the soft but contrasting colours. Nikon F3; 75 mm lens; 1/8 at f16; Kodachrome 64.

The urban landscape

Landscape photography has a rather romantic appeal and in most people's minds it conjures up images of rushing mountain streams, windswept meadows, and green valleys nestling between rolling hills. The urban environment is, however, just as rewarding and challenging a subject to a perceptive photographer, and an increasing number are choosing it as a source for their picture-making.

There are indeed some advantages in the urban subject. While even the most beautiful rural setting is dependent on subleties of lighting and cloud formations to reveal textures, shapes, and colours, the man-made contours of a city have more inherent graphic qualities which depend less on a trick of natural light than on the perception of the photographer and his ability to select an effective viewpoint to organize the elements of

Left Old and new are effectively juxtaposed in this shot of contrasting architectural styles, the light-toned pattern of the modern forming a foil for the almost silhouetted shape of the old. Pentax S1A; 135 mm lens; 1/125 at f8; Ilford FP4.

Opposite above Strong back lighting has emphasized the texture of the cobble-stones in this old corner of Copenhagen as well as contributing to the atmosphere of the picture. Pentax S1A; 55 mm lens; 1/125 at f8; Ilford FP4.

Opposite below The human figure emphasizes the rather strange juxtaposition of elements in this shot. A long-focus lens has also helped the effect by creating the impression of compressed perspective and isolating a small area of the scene. Pentax S1A; 200 mm lens; 1/250 at f8; Ilford FP4.

his picture. An urban setting can also contribute its own lighting qualities – street lighting, shop windows, fluorescent signs and displays all create atmosphere as well as adding a powerful visual element.

The approach to urban landscape photography can vary enormously from broad architectural vistas to the isolation of small details and textures just in the same way that rural landscape work can range from panoramic views to abstract images of rocks and trees, the essential difference being that the urban image consists of angular and geometric shapes and bold colour and tonal contrasts. Elements of design such as posters, signs, doors, telephone booths, and cars can all be used as the focal point or as an additional element in the composition.

People tend to be a more dominant element in urban landscapes than in rural settings and can help to create a sense of scale as well as adding interest and excitement to the picture; effective images can often be created by the juxtaposition of a human figure against the angular shape of a building or advertising billboards.

Junk objects

Beauty is said to be in the eye of the beholder and one of the good things about being a photographer is that it teaches you to see pleasing images in things or situations that other people would probably consider ugly or even offensive. For these photographers who like to 'find' their pictures and create abstract or graphic compositions by isolating aspects of a scene, junk objects can be a marvellous and rewarding subject.

In our society of instant obsolescence there is never a shortage of junk, and places like rubbish tips, auto wreckers, and derelict buildings are excellent sites for making good pictures. Rust, for instance, is wonderfully photogenic; it can create a rich and varied range of colours and textures, often unconsciously producing blends of colour and tone that an avant-garde painter would envy. Flaking paint, crumbling plaster, and rotting

timber also have the potential to create rich and powerful images.

The essence of such pictures is careful selection and precise framing. The choice of viewpoint can create a variety of juxtapositions and produce lighting effects which can emphasize the essential elements of the picture. Good technical quality is another vital ingredient; subtleties of texture, form, and colour require precise exposure and pin-sharp images. A tripod is an invaluable accessory since it enables small apertures to be used to obtain maximum depth of field and eliminates the possibility of camera shake as well as enabling the camera to be aimed and framed precisely. Using a long-focus lens will help you to isolate small areas of the scene and there is also the possibility of taking close-up pictures using extension tubes or macro lenses.

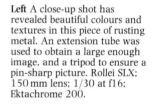

Left A close-up shot has revealed beautiful colours and textures in this piece of rusting metal. An extension tube was used to obtain a large enough image, and a tripod to ensure a pin-sharp picture. Rollei SLX; 150 mm lens; 1/30 at f16; Ektachrome 200.

Above right An almost abstract effect has been produced by isolating a small area of a piece of scrap metal, its shape emphasized by careful framing. Rollei SLX; 150 mm lens; 1/30 at f16; Ektachrome 200.

Above far right A weathered piece of wood on a derelict building has yielded an image with rich texture and interesting shapes. Nikon F2AS; 105 mm lens; 1/30 at f11; Orwo transparency film.

Right This tightly framed broken window has been juxtaposed against an open sky to give an almost surreal quality. Rollei SLX; 250 mm lens; 1/125 at f8; Ektachrome 64.

Shop windows

Shop windows may seem an odd subject for photography initially but if you begin to look at them with a selective eye you will find that they have much to offer, particularly to those who are interested in the more graphic photographic images. As a general rule it is a subject that has more potential for colour pictures, but black and white images can be equally effective under some circumstances.

The facias of a shop front have an inherently pleasing arrangement of shapes, with rectangles of different formats juxtaposed to form the doorway, the window, and the sign above. Within these rectangles all sorts of exciting things can happen. The sign can be a subject in itself: many older shops have ornate lettering while modern shop-fronts with their brash neon displays in primary colours can create a quite different effect. In addition to the signs above the windows there are often emblems and posters which can be incorporated into the picture.

The window display is an important feature although it is not always the most important aspect of the picture. Where it does form the centre of interest of the picture, however, it may be necessary to eliminate some of the reflections on the glass so that the objects inside can be clearly seen; a polarizing filter will usually be the most efficient means of doing this. In some cases the reflection can contribute to the picture by creating a multiple-image effect (pp. 66–7). Empty and even derelict shop-fronts where windows are painted over and doorways boarded up are another source of interesting images.

A straightforward approach is often the most effective with the window shot square on with little or no perspective. This can usually be done most easily by shooting from the opposite side of the street using a long-focus lens. Do not overlook the possibilities of shop-fronts at night and also of incorporating them with pictures of people.

Opposite below This multi-coloured shop-front was found in a Moroccan village. The central figure of the owner acts as a focal point in the chaos of colour. Nikon F3; 20 mm lens; 1/125 at f5.6; Ektachrome 64.

Left A single bold colour dominates this picture of a Soho shoe-mender's shop; the lettering and posters add to the composition. Nikon F2AS; 105 mm lens; 1/125 at f4; Ektachrome 64.

Below A close-up detail of a French boulangerie has provided an image in which the design of the window display and the sign-writer's art become the main point of interest. The reflection from the street in front has added a little to the picture without becoming too dominant. Nikon F3; 75 mm lens; 1/125 at f5.6; Ektachrome 64.

Reflected images

One way to create images with an unusual quality is to look for pictures and situations where you can photograph a reflected image of a subject instead of aiming your camera directly at it. This can produce a wide variety of effects, ranging from the subtle to the pure abstraction.

The success of this technique depends primarily on two factors: the availability of a suitable reflective surface and the correct balance of illumination between the subject and the reflective surface. Where, for instance, you have a smooth, highly reflective surface such as glass or metal and the subject itself is lit much more strongly, the result will be an almost perfect image of the scene. However, as the level of illumination in the reflective surface gets closer to that of the subject, so the image becomes more a combination of the two, resulting in pictures that have the same visual effect as a double exposure.

The nature of the surface will also have a dramatic effect on the reflection; it is quite possible, for instance, to obtain a near mirror-like reflection in the surface of still water but even a slight ripple will convert it to an abstraction of shapes and colours. There are essentially two approaches: one is

to combine the image of the subject with that of the surface in which it is being reflected, and the other is to use the surface to distort or modify the subject without being identifiable or noticeable in itself. In the first instance it is of course important that both the subject and the surface are in focus – in a distant scene such as landscape reflected in a lake this is not a problem but when the reflective surface is much closer to the camera than the object which is being reflected, then some thought must be given to focusing the camera so that both are recorded sharply.

To obtain optimum benefit from depth of field it is necessary to focus at a point one-third of the way between the nearest and furthest points which are required to be in focus. In most cases with this type of picture there will not be an actual object on which to focus and the best method is to measure the two distances, calculate the point one-third between them and set it manually on the lens. For maximum depth of field the smallest aperture should be used. A polarizing filter is a helpful accessory for this type of shot as it can be used to vary the strength of the reflected image; however, it will not have any effect on images reflected from metal surfaces.

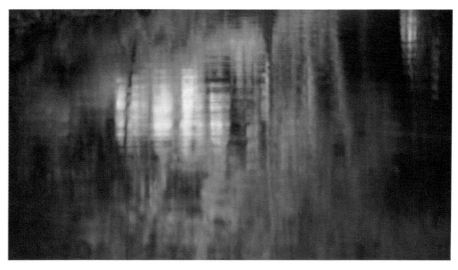

Left This almost abstract image
was made by photographing
the reflections of people and
trees at the side of a rippled
lake with the camera focused
on the reflection. Nikon F2;
150 mm lens; 1/60 at f4;
Kodachrome 64.

Above In this shot of Christmas
lights reflected in the wet
pavement the lens was focused
at a point to obtain both a
sharp foreground and
reflection. Nikon F3; 50 mm
lens; 1/30 at f11; Ektachrome
EL ISO 400/27°.

Right The distorted effect was
produced by photographing a
reflection of a sunlit building in
a window of poor-quality glass.
Nikon F3; 150 mm lens; 1/125
at f8; Ektachrome 64.

Street life

There are many good subjects which can provide a rewarding few hours or an afternoon for a photographer but are often neglected simply because they are so familiar and go unnoticed. A street is just one example which contains a rich and constantly changing source of pictures to be found by anyone who cares to look. Street life is very accessible even to a casual observer and a photographer who is interested in photographing people will not only find it full of activity and interest but will also discover that it is relatively easy for him to blend unobtrusively into the background and shoot unobserved.

There are many ways in which you can approach the photography of a street: for instance, it can be particularly challenging to set yourself the task of recording life in your own neighbourhood street where the effort of overcoming the blindness that familiarity induces can sometimes be more stimulating than the challenge of a completely unfamiliar environment. You could perhaps

Above right A street parade with a boys' band in Copenhagen has provided the setting for this shot of an eager young standard-bearer. A wide aperture and shallow depth of field have helped to isolate him from the background. Pentax S1A; 55 mm lens; 1/250 at f4; Kodak Tri-X.

Right One of the many forms of transport used on city streets, in this case Copenhagen. Nikon F; 35 mm lens; 1/250 at f8; Kodak Tri-X.

make a series of portraits of the individuals who live or work in the street – shopkeepers, cleaners, policemen – or you could make the assignment one in which you record the activities of the street through a period of time. Another approach would be to try to show the street in an unfamiliar way, say a city street at the week-end when it is shut up and deserted. Old photographs of streets in years gone by are very often of great interest, largely because a street more readily reflects the fashion and trends of the day and is an accurate measure of how things are changing both architecturally and socially. This can be another good approach to take, attempting to show the changes that are taking place within your own environment.

Transport and traffic are a vital aspect of street life and can be an important element of your pictures: cars, buses, bicycles, horses are all very photogenic, and the rush hour is a topic worthy of consideration all on its own. There are the street activities involving shops and markets, and in city environments you will come across street performers as well as more organized and formal entertainments such as processions and festivals.

Above The rush hour can provide good opportunities for pictures in the urban environment. A long-focus lens and tight framing have emphasized the crowded atmosphere of this shot. Nikon F; 150 mm lens; 1/250 at f5.6; Kodak Tri-X.

Left A shady spot in Barcelona's Ramblas has provided the setting for this shot; tight framing and a contrasting background have produced a bold image. Nikon F; 105 mm lens; 1/250 at f5.6; Kodak Tri-X.

Animal portraits

The majority of animal pictures are taken as full-length shots with the subject set against the background of its natural environment, but a very effective way of photographing animals, particularly the domestic or tame variety, is to shoot head-and-shoulder portraits in the same way that you would of a human subject. This has the advantage of focusing attention on the creature's face and emphasizing its expression, which frequently increases both the appeal and the impact of the picture.

In the case of small animals such as cats this will obviously involve quite close-up pictures and a long-focus lens will make things easier and more convenient; you will find at close focusing distances that a small aperture will be needed to ensure adequate depth of field. One advantage of tightly framed and close-up pictures is that distracting backgrounds can be subdued by being thrown well out of focus, and this will add further

emphasis to the animal's face and will heighten the impact.

This type of shot can be taken equally satisfactorily indoors or outdoors but indoor pictures will in most circumstances need some artificial lighting to enable the use of both a small aperture and a reasonably fast shutter speed to prevent subject movement. A portable flash is ideal, but if you aim it directly at the subject be careful that you do not get the 'red-eye' effect as a result of the flash being too close to the lens. Using the flash mounted on a bracket that holds it about a foot (30 centimetres) above or to one side of the lens will prevent this and at the same time create more modelling on the animal's face. Alternatively, the light from the flash can be bounced off a white ceiling or a reflector placed close to the subject. However, this will require an increase of exposure of 2 to 3 stops to compensate for the more widely scattered and diffused light.

Right The choice of a front-on viewpoint for this shot of a bull has helped to emphasize its aggressive appearance and purposeful gaze. Nikon F3; 105 mm lens; 1/125 at f8; Kodak Tri-X.

Left The appealing nature of this cat's expression has been exploited by very tight framing, with further impact from the dark background and shallow depth of field. The shot was taken using the light from a window indoors. Rollei SLX; 150 mm lens; 1/30 at f5.6; Kodak Tri-X.

Left The angle of the horse's head has created a strong diagonal composition which emphasizes the shape of the head. Nikon F3; 105 mm lens; 1/250 at f8; Ilford FP4.

71

People at work

One of the problems associated with photographing people is getting them to relax and behave in an unselfconscious way. The 'candid camera' approach is obviously one solution but it does have the disadvantage that the photographer has a more limited degree of control over the content and composition of the picture. An excellent compromise between the formal posed portrait and the unobserved shot is to photograph people at their work, and this can be equally satisfactory with both friends and strangers.

Most people feel somewhat vulnerable and self-conscious when confronted with a camera but the preoccupation with a familiar task and the surroundings of a personal environment invariably help them to act in a more relaxed and natural way. In addition,

the actual location can help the picture to say more about the personality and character of the subject than might the setting of a formal picture, as well as adding a considerable degree of interest.

Your approach can vary from quite close-up shots with just a suggestion of the person's occupation in the background or foreground, to pictures where the surroundings play a much more dominant role and the person you are photographing simply becomes one element in the total composition. In such cases, however, it is vital to organize the elements of the scene in such a way that the subject of the picture remains the focal point of the image while taking care that the background does not become a fussy and confusing distraction. Make sure that

Right These two workers on the dockside at Haifa have created an unselfconscious composition by the positions of their bodies and the chains they are handling. The brightly lit side of a boat has provided a contrasting background. Nikon F; 105 mm lens; 1/250 at f8; Ilford FP4.

Right This lady's magazine kiosk has been used as an important part of the composition in this informal portrait. Nikon F3; 105 mm lens; 1/250 at f5.6; Ilford XP1.

the subject is separated from the surroundings, either by juxtaposing him or her against
a contrasting tone or colour, or by using
lighting to create a tonal difference. You can
also make effective use of focusing
techniques so that the model is in sharp focus
but the background details are kept out of
focus, for instance by using a wide aperture
or a long-focus lens.

When shooting people in indoor situations
it is best to keep the lighting as simple as
possible in order to maintain the informal
atmosphere. You can use the light from a
window, from available light, or from a small
flash unit bounced from a ceiling.

As well as being a good way of producing
an individual portrait, the shot of a person at
work is also often a good approach for a picture story (pp.134–5) on the lines of 'A Day
in the Life of', for instance, or possibly as a
step-by-step sequence (pp.162–3).

Above The bold image of a
Spanish fisherman preoccupied
with his net relies on tight
framing and an uncluttered
background. Nikon F3;
105 mm lens; 1/250 at f8;
Ilford XP1.

Left A Welsh miner coming off
shift with his pit-pony has
made a good subject for this
posed but unselfconscious shot.
Nikon F2; 24 mm lens; 1/250
at f5.6; Kodak Tri-X.

Harbours

Picturesque fishing harbours are a popular and obvious subject for photography, but many photographers settle for a general view, often like a postcard shot. There is, however, considerable pictorial scope and the potential is just as great in the less obviously photogenic locations where the activity is more to do with cargo and industry than with casting a net. It is important to get permission before you start taking pictures, particularly in a large docks where customs or security regulations apply. In most cases, however, this is easily obtained.

The activities in a harbour are always visually interesting and varied; in a fishing harbour there is the landing of the catch, the mending of nets, and the repainting and repairing of boats. The machinery of a cargo harbour, with huge cranes and container hoists, will provide dramatic shapes and compositions. The human aspect also offers many opportunities. People occupied with strenuous tasks invariably make good pictures and are seldom camera-conscious, and you should not overlook the possibility of close-up character portraits as well as action shots.

Shapes are a dominant element in harbour pictures, the elegant lines of fishing-boats and yachts contrasting with the business-like and almost overwhelming structures of ocean-going craft and the dockside equipment that goes with them. There is opportunity here for interesting juxtapositions of shapes and outlines, and the effects of both telephoto and wide-angle lenses can be fully exploited. Take a closer view of such scenes as there is a rich variety of colour, texture, and pattern to be found in the vicinity of a harbour, from rusty cables and brightly painted cargo containers to greasy cogs and gleaming hulls, all elements that can be used to create rich tones and strong compositions.

Left In this shot of Honfleur in Normandy the bright sails and boats form an effective foil to the grey aspect of the distant buildings. Nikon F2AS: 24 mm lens; 1/25 at f8; Kodachrome 64.

Top This picture relies for its effect on tight framing and good composition as well as the colour contrast between the boat and the water. Pentax S1A; 135 mm lens; 1/250 at f8; Ektachrome 64.

Above A long-focus lens was used to create this juxtaposition. The exposure was calculated to record colour in the sun and to silhouette the crane. Nikon F3; 400 mm lens; 1/250 at f8; Ektachrome 200.

The zoo

Animals are ideal subjects for a photographer and have a very popular, almost universal appeal. With the exception of the domestic variety, however, they are also rather hard to find, apart that is from in a zoo, and an afternoon spent in a good zoo can provide a wealth of potential subjects for an observant photographer. In a conventional zoo, of course, the bars and cages are a restriction but with a little care and ingenuity in the framing of a picture it is possible to take shots that give little or no indication that the subject was in captivity.

A long-focus lens is a positive advantage: a lens of, say, 150–200 mm on a 35 mm camera can produce quite close-up images of larger animals from a considerable distance. A long-focus lens can also be used in conjunction with a fairly wide aperture to shoot through wire-mesh fence and make it 'disappear', providing the camera is quite close to the mesh and the animal is some distance from it. On the other hand, effective pictures

can be made using the bars and cages as an element of the composition, and even with a simple fixed-lens camera there are plenty of opportunities for good photographs.

It is worth while checking on the feeding times of the various animals because as well as making a good subject in itself the animals often disappear into their private quarters to sleep after feeding. At most zoos you will find that some animals are less restricted and even that some are allowed to wander around quite freely.

There are also of course the Wildlife and Safari Parks where the animals are kept in quite natural surroundings and you can take pictures from the observation points provided or from a car. When shooting from a car ensure that the window you are shooting through is spotlessly clean and hold your lens as close to it as possible. If the engine is running do not allow the camera to touch the glass as the vibration could result in a loss of sharpness in the image.

Far left A long-focus lens has helped to create this tightly framed shot of an elephant. Nikon F2; 200 mm lens; 1/250 at f8; Kodak Tri-X.

Left The bars of the tigers' cage have been used as a compositional element in this picture. Nikon F3; 105 mm lens; 1/60 at f5.6; Kodak Tri-X.

Above This quite natural setting for the shot of a stag was found in a Wildlife Park where there is often considerable scope for shooting pictures with sympathetic backgrounds. Nikon F3; 200 mm lens; 1/250 at f5.6; Ektachrome 64.

Right A compositional frame has added both impact and interest to this picture of giraffes. Nikon F2; 150 mm lens; 1/250 at f5.6; Kodak Tri-X.

The seaside

The seaside has a strong attraction for most people, and is in fact a place that many associate automatically with leisure and relaxation. Visually the seaside offers a rich variety of moods and vistas, and yet there are probably more boring pictures taken there than in any other setting! Like many locations that are on a grand scale it is probably the very vastness that makes it difficult for a photographer to 'see' pictures. The best approach is to 'think small' and look for the details and small corners which can easily get lost in the broader view. The variety of the landscape is itself vast, from deserted beaches to busy resorts, from rugged cliff scenery to the soft sand and tranquil waters of tropical islands.

In terms of diversity and colour an afternoon spent at a resort is hard to beat, especially for those who like to photograph people. Even the most retiring people tend to become rather more extrovert at the seaside, and the presence of a camera is unlikely to attract any attention, making it a simple matter to shoot unobserved. Most resorts, of whatever size, boast a fun-fair or pier, not to mention amusement arcades, beach huts, and perhaps donkey rides. Even the vulgarity of the souvenir stalls and entertainment stands has a striking visual quality that can provide pictorial inspiration. People tend to associate the seaside with sunshine but even on a dull or rainy day there is potential for taking good pictures. A seaside resort out of season has an atmosphere all its own, making it an ideal vehicle for a picture story or photo-essay.

Quite apart from the leisure aspects, many occupations are attached to the seaside, such as boat-building and fishing, and these can make ideal subjects for a photographer. The seaside is also an ideal location for more abstract and graphic pictures – rocks and rippled wet sand for instance, or textural shots of fishing boats and breakwaters. You will be able to find images with a strong element of pattern, rows of deckchairs or stacks of lobster pots. The pictorial potential of a day at the seaside is enormous once you have developed an eye for the details.

Opposite below Pattern and texture are the dominant elements of this tightly framed shot of crab pots which have been emphasized by the limited colour range. Nikon F3; 75 mm lens; 1/60 at f8; Kodachrome 64.

Left The colourfully painted doors of this row of beach huts and their reflection in the water provide an effective frame for the group of holiday-makers. A long-focus lens was used to isolate a small area of the scene. Nikon F3; 300 mm lens; 1/250 at f8; Kodachrome 64.

Left Shooting into the light has added impact to the image and texture to the surf in this seascape. A tobacco-coloured graduated filter was used to darken and add colour to the sky. Nikon F3; 20 mm lens; 1/250 at f11; Ektachrome 64.

79

A children's playground

Children are marvellous subjects for a photographer – expressive, extrovert, and unselfconscious – and they can produce pictures with a wide range of moods that have a universal appeal. A playground is an ideal location for photographs of children since these particular qualities are emphasized when children are together in a group.

There are many different sorts of playground, from an indoor pre-school nursery play group, to an adventure playground for older children in an urban development site. It is necessary and courteous to ask the relevant authority for permission to take photographs in any but a public place.

The first problem you are likely to encounter is that you will be surrounded by your potential subjects, doubtless pulling faces and begging to be photographed. This in itself may well provide good pictures since the unselfconscious spontaneity of children usually means that they will not 'play' to the camera in an unnatural way. At this stage you may feel that the opportunity to take unposed, candid pictures is non-existent, but you will invariably find that after you have taken a few shots the children will gradually become less interested and will return to their own preoccupations; after a while they will lose interest in the camera completely, leaving you free to shoot quietly and discreetly.

The most useful accessory will be a long-focus lens which will enable you to single out an individual child without having to

Right The children's totally uninhibited response has produced a picture with some charm in this shot taken in a school playground. A wide-angle lens and exaggerated perspective have helped to emphasize the lively atmosphere of the subject. Nikon F; 24 mm lens; 1/250 at f8; Kodak Tri-X.

Below right Concentration on their game has made the children quite unaware of the camera in this close-up shot. Nikon F; 105 mm lens; 1/250 at f5.6; Kodak Tri-X.

approach too closely, and will also enable you to separate him or her from what is likely to be a busy or cluttered background. You should choose your viewpoint carefully so that a suitable tone or colour is positioned behind the subject to provide a good contrast and help to isolate it from the surroundings.

In all photographs of people, and of children in particular, tight framing and the exclusion of extraneous details is most likely to produce the best results since it will emphasize the faces and expressions of your subjects. You will also find it necessary to use a fast shutter speed of say 1/250 sec to eliminate the possibility of camera shake and also to freeze the movement of your subjects as they play. For this reason, in all but the brightest lighting conditions you will find a fast film the best choice: ISO 200/24° with colour or ISO 400/27° with black and white.

Above Tight framing has emphasized the intent expression on this girl's face as she is caught in action while at play. Nikon F; 105 mm lens; 1/250 at f5.6; Kodak Tri-X.

Left An adventure playground has provided the setting for this shot of a child on a swing. Back lighting has helped to isolate her from the background which was included to add interest to the composition. Nikon F; 105 mm lens; 1/250 at f8; Kodak Tri-X.

The races

Any gathering of people creates a heightened, perhaps charged atmosphere, whether it is a protest meeting or a public performance, but few occasions offer a greater display of animation and interest than a day at the races. The races themselves are only one part of the visual aspect as far as a photographer is concerned, and there is a wealth of activity and human interest that will keep a camera clicking all afternoon. Meetings vary considerably from local affairs to formal, fashion-conscious gatherings such as Ascot in England or the Kentucky Derby in the United States. The advantage of smaller meetings is that the lack of formality offers greater freedom and choice of viewpoints, particularly where the actual races are concerned.

Choosing a good viewpoint is a vital consideration and it is good idea to select your

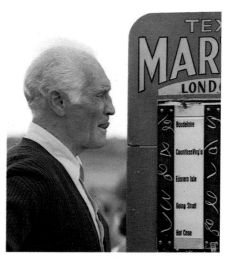

Top Candid shots like this one of a bookie are usually easy to find at a race meeting, given the variety of people and their preoccupation with the events. Nikon F2AS; 200 mm lens; 1/250 at f8; Ektachrome 64.

Above In this shot a long-focus lens was pre-focused on one spot and the shutter fired when the horses reached that point. Nikon F3; 400 mm lens; 1/500 at f5.6; Ektachrome 200.

Right The pattern of faces in the crowd has been emphasized by tight framing. Soft lighting from an overcast sky has avoided strong shadows. Nikon F3; 400 mm lens; 1/500 at f5.6; Ektachrome 200.

camera position in advance, perhaps asking the advice of a race official. Take the background into account when selecting a viewpoint; the faces of the crowd in the grandstand would be more pleasing than a row of parked cars. A long-focus lens is a distinct advantage as it allows a wider choice of viewpoint, and the shallow depth of field will help to subdue what can be unduly fussy backgrounds. Although the finishing line is a popular choice of viewpoint, a turn or, at a steeple-chase, a jump, can often provide a more exciting location.

In addition to the actual race do not forget to look out for shots of people reacting to the tension and excitement. A race meeting is invariably populated with colourful characters such as bookies and tipsters who usually tend to be photogenic. The horses are prime subjects, and the preparations for the race and the parading of horses in the paddock all represent good opportunities for pictures.

The market

For the photographer who likes to take a candid, unobserved approach to photographing people there are few better venues than a market. To begin with, there are invariably plenty of people, and a lot of activity and a general preoccupation with buying and selling that make the presence of a photographer less obvious and intrusive. Market people themselves are also usually quite extrovert and markets are often well populated with the sort of individuals and 'characters' that make ideal photographic subjects.

Certain countries such as Britain and France have a long tradition of market-trading and almost every town will be able to offer the visiting photographer a suitable location, from a fruit and vegetable market in a street to an indoor antiques market. In large cities like London, Paris, and New York there are markets which take over whole neighbourhoods, spilling into every small street and alley-way.

In photographic terms the one thing that is common to all markets is a profusion of detail and the main problem for a photographer is to isolate his subject from this confusion and arrange the elements of the image into a pleasing and balanced composition. One way of doing this is simply to move in close and frame the picture quite tightly. If you are taking an individual person as the main subject of the picture where the face and expression is of great importance then this is the best solution. By using a long-focus lens at a fairly wide aperture the limited depth of field will enable the subject to be separated clearly from the background and will at the same time allow you to work at a reasonable distance from the subject and so be less obtrusive. When a wider view is required great care must be taken to avoid a confusion of details; the choice of viewpoint and the framing of the image should be made in such a way that there is a clearly definable centre of interest around which the other elements of the image are balanced.

Lighting can be a problem as well as there is usually a drastic change in brightness levels between various parts of the scene, for instance under covered stalls in an open market. This must be taken into consideration when choosing a viewpoint as the shadows and the highlights which are created are also potentially confusing and can be a hazard to successful composition. You should frame your pictures so that the image is predominantly in either shadow or highlight areas and calculate the exposure accordingly, avoiding pictures where there is an even mixture of the two.

Below This slightly bizarre image was found at a clothes stall in a country market. Tight framing has accentuated the pattern. Nikon F3; 105 mm lens; 1/250 at f8; Kodak Tri-X.

Below left The droplets of water on this 'found' still life of peppers taken during a rain-shower have added texture and sparkle to the already dominant pattern. Nikon F3; 105 mm lens; 1/125 at f5.6; Ilford FP4.

Above right A quiet corner of the flea market in Paris provided the opportunity for this candid picture which depends for its success as much on its composition as on its subject. Rolleicord; 1/125 at f4; Ilford FP4.

Right Market people are often extrovert, making possible spontaneous and uninhibited pictures such as this one in a Spanish street market. Rolleicord; 1/125 at f5.6; Ilford FP4.

The park

Most towns have a park of some sort, be it a simple recreational area with a playground for children and a few benches or a vast wooded and landscaped area like London's Hyde Park. A park is a marvellous place for photography for a number of reasons. Because it is a place of leisure and relaxation there are always people – feeding ducks, sitting on benches, listening to bands, jogging – making it an ideal situation in fact for those who prefer the candid unobserved approach to photographing people. There is also a sense of order and an inherent formality about a park which aids composition and

helps a photographer to create organized and well-balanced pictures. A further bonus is that parks, particularly city parks, are usually full of objects such as benches and deck-chairs, little kiosks, ponds, lakes, fountains, statues, all of which can be used as decorative and pictorial elements in a picture. Some parks like the Tuillerie Gardens in Paris contain such elegant and attractive structures that it is almost impossible not to find interesting pictures.

Each park has its own character and the pictures you take in one park are likely to be totally different from those you might take in

Above Many parks have space for people to play games and to exercise, giving the photographer opportunities for action shots like this one of early-morning joggers on Hampstead Heath in London. Nikon F2AS; 24 mm lens; 1/250 at f8; Kodak Tri-X.

Right Feeding the birds is a popular activity, and often makes an appealing subject for a photographer, as this shot in a Parisian park demonstrates. Nikon F2AS; 210 mm lens; 1/250 at f8; Kodak Tri-X.

another. There is almost always something happening in a park at any time of day and at any season, and in fact a local park would make an ideal 'source subject' to which you can return again and again, even taking the same subject under different conditions of light and time. Many photographers have a pet theme like this and it means you always have somewhere to go for an hour or two.

A park would be an ideal subject for a photo-essay or a picture series. Apart from being a good subject in itself a park can often provide an ideal location for glamour photographs perhaps, or provide backgrounds for a portrait session where the more formal settings may be more suitable and more varied than open countryside.

Above Small details can create images with a graphic or abstract quality as in this shot of a park bench surrounded by an almost geometrically trimmed hedge. Nikon F2AS; 70 mm lens; 1/60 at f8; Ilford FP4.

Left The formalized landscaping in city parks often means that there is an inherent composition, making it easier to find well-organized and balanced pictures. This one was taken in Copenhagen. Nikon F; 105 mm lens; 1/250 at f8; Kodak Tri-X.

87

Railways

The railway has a strong, almost romantic attraction for some people and since much of this attraction is visual this makes it a stimulating subject for photographers. It is of course the steam engine which produces the greatest nostalgic response in most people, and although the old engines are being phased out they are still in operation in some places and are also maintained and operated by various preservation societies. The headquarters of these societies can provide an ideal opportunity for photography at close range, especially as they usually have sidings full of old engines and rolling stock in various stages of renovation. There is considerable scope here for detail shots in which the shape, texture, and colours of the machinery can be exploited by isolating and emphasizing small aspects of the subject by means of careful framing and composition. A long-focus lens and a tripod are a considerable asset in this type of shot since they enable you to have precise control over focusing and framing as well as ensuring that you achieve a pin-sharp image.

The track itself can provide plenty of pictorial possibilities, from a busy junction in an urban setting to a small single track curving its way through a piece of deserted countryside. The perspective effects of converging

lines can be exploited to the full, adding to the impression of depth and distance in a landscape and creating bold compositions. There is also ample opportunity for creating strong patterns which can be emphasized by the use of both wide-angle and long-focus lenses.

In addition to the track and the rolling stock there is also considerable potential in the architecture and equipment of the railway: level crossings, bridges, signals, freight yards, and stations themselves all make interesting and varied photographic subjects. Apart from the actual railway settings there is also of course a great deal of opportunity for human interest pictures. A subject such as the rush hour in an urban environment would make an ideal vehicle for a picture story or photo-essay.

Far left Railway equipment and machinery can often be ideal subjects for pictures dependent on shapes and textures such as this close-up of rolling stock. Nikon F3; 105 mm lens; 1/60 at f11; Ilford FP4.

Above Railway tracks have a strong graphic quality which can be used to create bold compositions. This winding stretch of line gives a strong sense of depth. Nikon F3; 75 mm lens; 1/125 at f11; Ilford XP1.

Left Steam trains invariably provide a subject with both atmosphere and interest. This shot was taken at a steam enthusiasts' open day. Nikon F3; 105 mm lens; 1/125 at f8; Ilford FP4.

The farm

An afternoon spent on a farm offers a wide range of possible photographic subjects. You will of course have to obtain the farmer's permission, but if you make the right approach and perhaps offer a few prints in return it is unlikely that you will be refused. There are many different types of farm from just a few acres to large-scale co-operatives; a smallholding with varied livestock, for instance, would be an ideal place to shoot animal portraits (pp. 70–1). There are many activities on a farm involving animals which can make good subjects for photography – herding sheep with a dog, for example, or the milking shed – and many smaller farms still use horses for work as well as transport; a Shire horse with all its trappings is a truly photogenic subject. Machinery on a farm is also worthy of attention: ploughs, threshing machines, combine harvesters, and farm carts all present pictorial possibilities with their interesting shapes and textures.

On a practical level do not forget that even in dry weather most farms tend to be muddy and a pair of gum-boots should be considered vital equipment. Country crafts are not all dead and buried, indeed many are alive and well and are practised on farms. It is worth talking to local people and making enquiries at the nearest library. Hurdle making, thatching, cheese and butter making, dry-stone walling, and hedging are all fascinating and photogenic skills and would make ideal subjects for a step-by-step series (pp. 162–3) or a picture story (pp. 134–5) as well as providing subjects for individual pictures. Farms are of course also ideal locations for taking portraits of people at work.

A farm is often a good place to combine human subjects with landscape; activities like ploughing and harvesting can give strong photographic images where the human interest and natural setting are successfully combined.

Far left A farm is often a good location for pictures which combine human interest and landscape, as is seen in this photograph of harvesters in the Austrian Tyrol. Pentax S1A; 55 mm lens; 1/125 at f5.6; Kodachrome 25.

Above Old and worn farm equipment often provides good opportunities for pictures rich in shapes and textures, like this cartwheel. Nikon F2; 105 mm lens; 1/60 at f5.6; Kodachrome 25.

Left Horses are still used for farm work, even in Western countries, and make interesting photographic subjects. Nikon F3; 150 mm lens; 1/125 at f8; Ektachrome 64.

Waterways

Water holds a fascination for many people and its visual qualities make it a particularly effective element in a photograph. Its movement and response to light and the sky can create subtle tones and colours and its reflective qualities can add considerable impact to a picture. Apart from its visual qualities, however, water in the form of rivers and canals also influences our lives considerably, creating industry, transport, and architecture for instance, and this aspect of water can also be an absorbing and rewarding subject.

Boats and barges are obvious photographic examples of waterway transport but in addition to these there are also bridges, locks, and aqueducts which can provide scope for a wide variety of pictures from close-up details of machinery to architectural pictures and

Right The soft, almost smoke-like quality of the water in this shot of a mountain waterfall has been created by the use of a slow shutter speed, giving added contrast to the jagged granite rock. Nikon F3; 150 mm lens; 2 at f22; Ilford XP1; polarizing filter to reduce the exposure reading.

landscapes. Exploring a stretch of river would form an ideal subject for a picture story showing the changes that take place in the countryside through which it passes – the towns and villages along its banks and the activities and industries that occupy it.

On a more abstract level it is interesting to look at the photographic possibilities in moving water such as weirs and waterfalls or fast-flowing streams, and to experiment with the effects that can be created by using different shutter speeds, short exposures such as 1/250 sec or 1/500 sec to 'freeze' the movement, and long exposures of up to several seconds to create blur.

The leisure aspects of waterways can also offer good pictorial opportunities: sailing and canoeing make effective subjects for sport and action photography, and a lone fisherman can provide an effective focal point in a landscape picture. A river is an ideal location for nature and wildlife photography, and shooting from a boat is often a useful way of providing both cover and access.

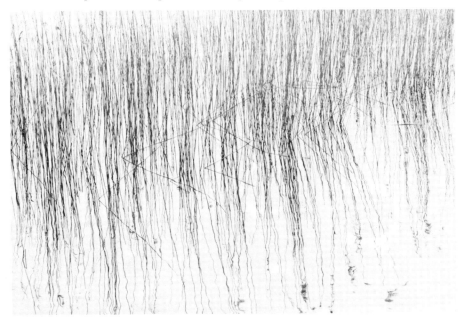

Above A tightly framed detail of reeds at the edge of a river has produced an almost abstract effect in this shot. Nikon F2AS; 105 mm lens; 1/30 at f11; Ilford FP4; tripod.

Left This French canal with its tree-lined banks has provided a good subject for a peaceful landscape shot which has been emphasized by the soft and slightly misty quality of the light. Nikon F3; 150 mm lens; 1/60 at f11; Ilford FP4.

93

Industry

'Photogenic' and 'picturesque' are words which sum up the conventional approach to photography and many photographers only react to scenes which they find attractive or pretty. However, the camera used by a photographer with a perceptive eye can reveal images of considerable beauty in subjects that superficially seem quite unattractive. There can even be some pleasure in doing this, since anyone can see the beauty in an autumn woodland scene but it takes a photographer's eye to find it in the less appealing aspects of our environment.

Few people live beyond the reach of industry, and the industrial aspects of the countryside can in fact provide considerable potential for picture-making. Large industrial complexes such as steelworks or coalmines have pictorial qualities on the scale of a landscape; indeed they often have their own particular lighting qualities as the result

of smoke and pollution, aspects which although environmentally undesirable can create effective photographic images. This type of industry also provides images where dramatic shapes and dynamic lines are dominant elements and quite stark bold compositions can be created. Some of the very old factories still exist and still function, and the passage of time has given these an aesthetic quality bordering on the picturesque.

A visit to your local industrial archaeological sites could produce pictures of quite dramatic contrast to those of modern installations. Do not forget to take a closer look at the machines; these are ideal sources of pattern and texture, and quite abstract images can be produced by isolating small details from a scene. Bold compositions using colour can also be created in the same way. This type of picture is much more dependent on how you see rather than what you see.

Far left Back lighting has created the dramatic effect in this shot of a steelworks, silhouetting the chimneys and emphasizing the clouds of smoke. A long-focus lens has isolated a small area of the scene. Nikon F2AS; 300 mm lens; 1/60 at f11; Ilford FP4.

Above left The complex shapes in this pit-head wheel have been carefully framed against a blank sky; the building in the lower right corner helps to balance the arrangement. Nikon F2AS; 135 mm lens; 1/125 at f5.6; Ilford FP4.

Above right The tightly framed picture of a winch uses bold highlights to emphasize the shape and texture of the subject. Nikon F3; 105 mm lens; 1/60 at f8; Ilford FP4.

Left Disused machinery has been used as a foreground element in this shot of a Welsh mining valley, increasing the impression of depth and distance. Nikon F2AS; 70 mm lens; 1/15 at f16; Ilford FP4.

The circus

There are few entertainments as colourful and photogenic as a circus and it is well worth the trouble of locating and travelling to one, as the potential for good photography is considerable. It is important, however, to ask permission of the circus authorities first if you want to take more than a casual snapshot. You may well find that opportunities and facilities will be offered to you that would not be possible without the willing co-operation of the performers.

Quite apart from the actual performance a circus offers a wealth of interest and activity

long before the audience arrives. With a touring circus, for instance, the erection of the big top is an exciting and colourful event in itself and much of the equipment and fittings are also very photogenic as they are usually painted in traditional bright colours, while even the insignia on trucks and caravans have temptingly pictorial qualities.

A few hours spent behind the scenes as the circus is setting up will yield a considerable variety of possible pictures. You may be able to capture the preparations for the performance – the animals being fed or assembled, for

Right This portrait of a clown was one of a series taken of him making-up in his caravan. The lighting was from the window diffused by net curtains, one of which provided the white background. Nikon F3; 105 mm lens; 1/60 at f5.6; Kodak Tri-X.

example – and you may even manage to persuade the artistes to let you shoot some portraits as they make-up or when they are in costume.

The performance itself is of course what most people want to photograph, and like many other forms of indoor entertainment the main problems are viewpoint and lighting. A ringside seat is obviously an advantage but at the same time you will not be able to vary your viewpoint once you have taken your place. A long-focus lens will in any event be a useful accessory to enable you to make tightly framed pictures.

Whether you are shooting in black and white or colour you will need a fast film, ISO 400/27° for instance, and it may well be necessary to uprate it to 800/30° or even 1600/33° by push-processing, particularly when you are using a long-focus lens which has a relatively small maximum aperture. In making the exposure calculation you should take into account the high contrast produced by spotlighting; a good method is to take an average reading from the lightest and darkest parts of the scene. In the case of close-up shots you should take particular care to frame the picture so that extremes of brightness are avoided, and also make sure that the light sources themselves are excluded from the meter's field of view to avoid the possible risk of under-exposure.

Left A brief rest during the unloading of the circus equipment gave rise to this informal portrait of a performer. Nikon F3; 105 mm lens; 1/125 at f8; Kodak Tri-X.

Above left A long-focus lens was used to isolate these high-wire performers from the rest of the action, emphasizing their expressions and preventing the picture from becoming too busy. Nikon F3; 200 mm lens; 1/60 at f4; Kodak Ektachrome tungsten film rated at ISO 400/27°.

Above right The bold colours and designs which are part of the circus tradition make effective elements in a composition, as the big top in the background of this shot shows. Nikon F3; 105 mm lens; 1/125 at f5.6; Ektachrome 64.

Right A long-focus lens was used in this ringside shot to capture an exciting moment in the performance. Nikon F2; 80 mm lens; 1/125 at f4; Ektachrome 200.

Style and Approach

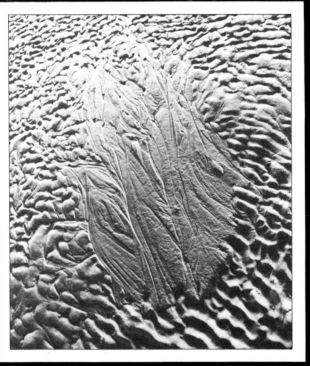

A touch of humour

Most people respond well to a picture which has an element of humour or wit, and indeed such pictures are sought after by newspapers and magazines. The best pictures of this type, however, are invariably those that are found rather than created, and the deliberately contrived photograph must be done very well indeed if it is not to appear corny or banal. Nevertheless a good idea which is carefully planned and well executed can produce genuinely funny results, and when a picture is taken for personal use such as a greetings card or a calendar you can make use of private jokes and you can caricature individual habits or behaviour.

There is also a 'half-way' approach where a potentially funny situation can be exploited by a degree of contrivance – a 'Beware of the Dog' notice could be used as a background for a shot of a cat nonchalantly cleaning itself or of a tiny dog gripping a piece of torn clothing

Above right Having spotted a potentially humorous situation, all that was necessary was to wait until a passer-by provided an effective juxtaposition and expression. Rolleicord; 1/125 at f5.6; Ilford FP4.

Right The humour in this shot found in a French market comes from the combination of the man's rounded profile and the arrangement of eggs on the car roof. Nikon F3; 150 mm lens; 1/125 at f8; Kodak Tri-X.

Opposite above Back views of people often have a humorous element as shown in this man's rather furtive attitude. Hasselblad; 150 mm lens; 1/250 at f5.6: Kodak Tri-X.

Opposite below This shot depends on both the juxtaposition and scale of the dog and its human companions, and the plain background which throws the subjects into bold relief. Nikon F2AS; 200 mm lens; 1/250 at f8; Kodak Tri-X.

in its teeth. An amusing image often results from juxtapositions of this type or when things are shown in an unfamiliar context. It requires both an observant eye and the right attitude of mind to see such pictures but, like other areas of photography, once you have started to look for and identify this type of image they will appear more frequently.

Humour is also often a little cruel, and photography lends itself very well to exploiting the unconscious and often undignified actions of people when they think they are unobserved. The line between what is funny and what is simply unkind is sometimes a hard one to draw and is something that will be decided by a photographer's own taste and approach and that of his audience. For this type of shot, however, you will need not only a keen eye but complete familiarity with your equipment so that you can react spontaneously to a situation. Framing, focusing, and exposing must be a swift, smooth, and unconscious operation as you will seldom get the chance for a second shot.

Bad weather

Many photographers never consider taking pictures in poor weather conditions and this means that they lose many opportunities of creating images with both atmosphere and subtle and unusual lighting effects. In outdoor photography the quality of the light is governed largely by atmospheric conditions – hard directional light on a sunny day with blue sky, for instance, and a softer light when there are clouds – but there are also other conditions which can affect both the quality of light and the subject itself, such as mist and snow, and these can often give rise to some of the most effective images.

In landscape photography mist and fog can literally create a picture by subduing background details and allowing foreground elements to be isolated from their surroundings, and in addition the presence of mist in a picture often helps to create mood. Even a small degree of atmospheric haze can contribute greatly to a picture, for instance by reducing the contrast in a sunset shot.

Exposure must be calculated precisely since under-exposure will create a grey muddy effect and over-exposure will lose vital highlight details; a good method is to take an average from the lightest and darkest areas of the scene. In black and white pictures a blue filter can be used to emphasize the effect of mist. Snow can help to simplify a scene by emphasizing shapes and lines and isolating details. However, exposure can be a problem when taking pictures of a snow scene, and the safest method is to take a close-up reading from a mid-tone or a shadow and not from the snow itself.

Pictures taken in the rain often benefit from the 'sparkle' that is produced by the highlights created on wet surfaces; this can be particularly effective in shots of street scenes at night for instance. The effect of falling rain can also often give a pleasingly soft, almost textured, effect. Remember, however, to protect your camera as much as possible from the effects of moisture and to dry it thoroughly with a soft cloth when you have finished shooting.

Left Fog has created a delicate
pastel quality in this shot of a
tree-lined avenue, subduing
background details and
emphasizing the shapes of the
trees. Nikon F3; 75 mm lens;
1/60 at f8; Ektachrome 64.

Below Thunderstorms often
create dramatic lighting
conditions for landscape
photography, as this shot of a
Highland loch demonstrates.
Nikon F3; 75 mm lens; 1/60 at
f8; Ektachrome 64.

Top The slight blue cast of this
picture shot at dusk after a
snowstorm in the Vosges
mountains helps to emphasize
the bleak atmosphere of the
scene. Nikon F3; 75 mm lens;
1/8 at f5.6; Ektachrome 200.

Above The red-striped hut adds
interest to this picture taken
during a heavy snowstorm. A
longish shutter speed has
helped to record the falling
snow. Rollei SLX; 150 mm lens;
1/4 at f16; Ektachrome 200.

103

Using shadows

A shadow is usually considered simply as a variation in tone within the subject, as a product of directional lighting which contributes to the solidity of the image. However, shadows can be used as a much more dominant element of the picture and can add to the composition of the image in the same way as objects and details within the scene. Shadows can also lend a quality of mood and drama to a photograph, either by creating strong shapes or lines or by obscuring parts of the subject and introducing an element of the mysterious. In movie-making, film directors invariably make a conscious and controlled use of shadows when they want to introduce or heighten the sense of drama or tension in a scene.

Shadows are more easily controlled where studio lighting is used; even the simple expedient of allowing the lighting to cast a shadow of the subject on to the background can create interesting effects when done in a controlled way although in normal circumstances it is to be avoided. Shadows can add excitement to a plain background by using a stencil cut from a piece of black card with a narrow beam light such as a spotlight to project the shadows on the background; horizontal slits can be cut in the card to create the effect of a venetian blind for instance. To obtain a more clearly defined effect you can paint the pattern on a piece of clear film with photopaque or cut pieces of black adhesive tape, and use it in a slide projector as if it were a transparency.

In outdoor situations you will be largely dependent on bright sunlight to create your shadow effects since dense, well-defined shadows are only created under these conditions. Shooting into the light, for instance, will often produce dramatic shadow effects which when the sun is low in the sky will be projected forwards towards the camera. Do not forget to make adequate allowance for deep shadows when you are calculating exposure; you should ignore the shadow area when taking the reading as otherwise overexposure will result.

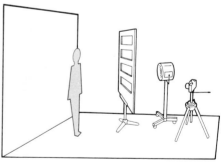

Left This picture is almost totally dependent on the shadows cast by the columns for its content, and their bold pattern creates a feeling of depth. Pentax S1A; 55 mm lens; 1/125 at f8; Ilford FP4.

Below The single strong shadow cast by the back-lit street sign becomes a dominant element in the composition of this image of shapes and textures. Nikon F2; 105 mm lens; 1/125 at f11; Ilford FP4.

The illustration shows how a card stencil or screen can be used to throw a shadow pattern on to the background. The lighting used for the model must be screened from the background to prevent the shadow effect from being weakened or lost.

Far left A shadow pattern on the background has created an additional compositional element in this portrait as well as helping to establish a mood. It was produced by the method shown in the illustration. Rollei SLX; 150 mm lens; 1/30 at f5.6; Kodak Tri-X.

Romantic glamour

There are many approaches to the photography of women, but one of the most enduring styles, and also the most flattering, is the soft romantic imagery which photographers like David Hamilton and Sarah Moon have perfected. To a large extent this type of picture tends to idealize women, thereby creating an impression which relies more upon fantasy than reality. The various photographic techniques which can help to convey this romantic mood are those which make the picture look less photographic and therefore less real.

The most basic method is to reduce the ability of the modern high-definition lenses to record every detail with such stark clarity, where every blemish and pore is revealed. This is most simply done by the use of the soft focus attachments made by many manufac-

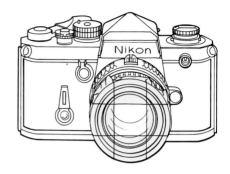

Above To create soft focus effects, adhesive tape can be stretched across the front of the lens (top); or (below) petroleum jelly smeared on a filter.

Left Although taken in harsh Mediterranean sunlight, softness was achieved by positioning the model in an area of open shade. Rollei SLX; 150 mm lens; 1/125 at f5.6; Kodak Ektachrome 64.

Right Soft lighting and harmonious colours have produced this effect. Adhesive tape was stretched over the lens. Pentax 6 × 7; 150 mm lens; 1/125 at f5.6; Kodak Ektachrome 200.

Far right Shooting into the light and the use of a soft focus attachment have resulted in a pleasing lighting quality. Nikon F3; 105 mm lens; 1/125 at f5.6; Kodak Ektachrome 64; Softar attachment.

turers. This has the double advantage of reducing the definition of the lens, so that skin is recorded as a smooth flawless tone, and of creating a pleasing spread of highlights into the darker tones to produce a halo-like quality, most effectively when the subject is back-lit. In addition to the manufactured attachments there is a variety of equally effective home-made devices such as clear adhesive tape stretched across a lens hood or petroleum jelly smeared on to a UV filter. It is important with these methods to leave a clear spot in the centre of the lens to permit a degree of sharpness to be retained.

In addition to soft focus techniques it is equally, if not more, important to ensure that your subject is 'soft' in other ways; for example, the lighting should be soft so that bright highlights and dense shadows are avoided, and the model's clothes should be selected so that strong colour or tonal contrasts are avoided. You should aim to

produce an image with a harmonious colour quality with hues that blend rather than those which react against each other. It is generally best to avoid clothes or fabrics with bold patterns or textures and the same should apply to the choice of settings and backgrounds. Another effective means of reducing both the contrast and colour separation of an image is by the use of a fog or pastel filter; a less controllable but similar effect can be created by breathing on the lens to 'mist' it over slightly.

Choice of film can also help the mood of the picture. As a general rule the faster colour films tend to have lower contrast and colour saturation than the slower types and in addition the coarser grain structure of the fast films such as Ektachrome 400 and others can help to 'break up' the image and add a pleasing quality. This effect can be further enhanced by shooting the film at a higher ASA speed and push-processing.

Framing the image

Composition is the technique of organizing and arranging the elements of a picture into a balanced and unified image. There are a number of devices which will help to achieve this, using lines of perspective to lead the eye into the picture for instance, or placing the main point of interest on the intersection of thirds to create the greatest impact. One 'trick' which can be used in a variety of ways and in different circumstances to create a harmonious composition is to find some element within the scene you are photographing which can be used to form a frame around the image. It does not necessarily have to be all round the image but could be just along the top or along one side and the base. The most common example of this use of a frame is probably the picture in which the overhanging branch of a tree creates an arch over a landscape shot; as well as helping to 'contain' the picture this can often be an effective way of masking a flat, uninteresting sky tone. An archway or doorway can be used in a similar way as a frame in an arch-itectural shot or an urban landscape.

In addition to being a helpful device in terms of composition the use of a frame in this type of picture can help to produce a feeling of depth and distance in a photograph. Although the most obvious use of this technique is as a foreground detail in a shot of a quite distant subject, it can also be used to good effect in portrait or still-life photography. For example, your model can be positioned behind a window or inside a doorway and in close-up shots the model's arms can be positioned so that they create the frame.

In the studio it is possible to use lighting to create a frame effect – a small spotlight can be positioned behind the subject and directed at the background to create a pool of light behind the model so that the darker tones create the frame effect towards the edges of the picture. The frame technique is worth considering when you have a picture lined up in your viewfinder which seems to be a little lacking in some way; it can often be the answer to the problem.

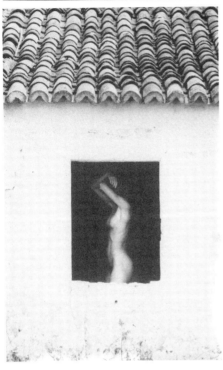

Left The foreground frame has been used to arrange the elements of the image and help to create a three-dimensional effect. Nikon F3; 105 mm lens; 1/250 at f8; Ilford XP1.

Above left A window in a derelict farmhouse has added impact and a degree of intrigue to this nude shot. Rollei SLX; 250 mm lens; 1/125 at f8; FP4.

Above right The view towards the Dead Sea from the ruined fortress of Massada has gained an extra impression of height and distance from the use of the silhouetted foreground frame. Nikon F3; 28 mm lens; 1/125 at f8; FP4.

Right The effect of this shot of the cathedral at Barcelona has been increased by using the overhanging branches of a tree as a frame. Hasselblad; 50 mm

Heads in close-up

The majority of portrait photographs, both formal and informal, include at least some proportion of the model's body. Even if only the shoulders are included it means that the model's head only represents about a third of the picture area, and when the picture also includes the arms the head will occupy only a relatively small area of the image. Consequently, when a picture is framed in such a way that the model's head occupies all or nearly all of the picture the impact is considerable, and when this is combined with a strong face, an appealing expression, and good lighting the result can be a very powerful photograph.

The standard approach to the composition of a portrait can no longer be applied in such a case since instead of the actual head itself being the centre of interest one particular aspect of the face must dominate the image; in normal circumstances this will be the eyes, but the mouth too can become the focal point. Once you decide that you can exclude the model's body it can also be useful to think in terms of cropping into the model's head as this can give a different emphasis to both the composition and the mood of the picture. Even though you are framing so tightly it does not eliminate the possibility of a hand or even just a few fingers being introduced into the picture in order to add a further element of interest.

Lighting considerations are no different from a conventional portrait except of course that strong shadows on the face will be more dominant as will the textural quality of directional lighting, but emphasis is the main purpose of this type of portrait. The main technical difficulty is depth of field which will be more limited at closer focusing distances, while a small aperture will be needed to ensure that the head is sharp from front to back. As a general rule it is best to focus on the eyes but when a three-quarter-face shot is taken it is best to focus on the nose or mouth.

When working with a standard lens beware of unpleasant perspective effects produced by shooting from a close viewpoint – this will be more noticeable with full-face pictures and when shooting from above or below the model's eye level; with three-quarter-face and profile shots the problem is not so acute. A long-focus lens is an invaluable accessory as it allows you to create a tightly framed picture without having to shoot from too close a viewpoint.

Right The choice of a landscape format, combined with tight framing and the off-centre composition, has emphasized the man's purposeful expression. Nikon F2; 150 mm lens; 1/15 at f11; Ilford FP4; tripod.

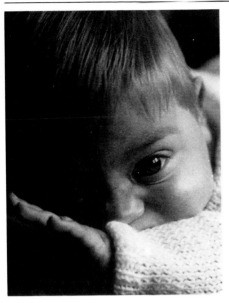

Above left Close cropping has added impact to the baby's eyes in this portrait and created an intimate atmosphere. Pentax SIA; 135 mm lens; 1/60 at f5.6; Kodak Tri-X.

Above right The inclusion of the man's hand in the picture aids the composition at the same time as accentuating his quizzical expression and utilizing a personal characteristic. Nikon F3; 150 mm lens; f11 with studio flash; Ilford FP4.

Right The impact of the model's eyes and mouth in this full-face portrait has been heightened by the tight framing and soft lighting. A texture screen was used during the printing to subdue skin texture. Nikon F3; 150 mm lens; f11 with studio flash; Ilford FP4.

111

Silhouettes

A silhouette is the most basic type of image and yet it can produce an instantly identifiable reproduction of a subject. Looking for and shooting silhouettes is an excellent way of developing a keen eye for the fundamental elements of a picture and also of learning the skills of composition. In its simplest form, a silhouette is a black shape on a white background and even this can produce an effective image with a subject that has an interesting outline. A pure silhouette can be created most easily by studio lighting techniques. One method is to place a tracing-paper screen close to the subject, between subject and camera, and to project a silhouette on to the screen by placing a spotlight or a slide projector behind the subject aimed towards the camera. Another method is to aim one or two studio lights at a white background, with the subject in front of it, ensuring that the illumination is restricted to the background and does not spill on to the subject.

Above The diagrams show two ways of creating a silhouette. (Left) With the model well in front of a white background the lights are aimed at the background, ensuring that no stray light spills on the subject. (Right) The model is close to a tracing-paper screen with the camera in front of it; a light source is aimed from behind the model towards the screen to cast a sharp shadow.

Left Shooting into the light and calculating the exposure for detail in the sky has allowed the foreground and building to record as a near-black tone. Nikon F3; 70 mm lens; 1/250 at f11; Ilford FP4.

Another effective way of shooting a silhouette which does not involve the use of lighting equipment is to position the subject inside an open door or window and to shoot from the inside. In all instances it is important to calculate the exposure so that it is sufficient to produce a good clean white but not enough to record detail on the subject itself. A good way of doing this is to take a reading from the white background and to increase the exposure by 2 to 3 stops.

In outdoor situations a silhouette can be achieved in several ways. One is to shoot from a low viewpoint so that your subject is outlined against the sky and to give minimal exposure as described. Another method is to position the subject in an area of deep shade and select a viewpoint that enables a brightly lit area of the surroundings to act as a background. A silhouette obviously does not have to be pure black and white as long as the foreground subject is very dark and any detail is not obtrusive. The effect will still be striking when the background area has some tone or colour. When shooting in colour it can be effective to use a quite strong colour filter to add colour to a blank sky.

Above Studio lighting has been used to create a silhouette in this nude picture; two lights were directed at a white background and were screened to prevent spill on to the model. Nikon F3; 105 mm lens with studio flash; Ilford FP4.

Left This shot of a tattered screen built to protect a hop-field from the wind has been given an almost abstract quality by silhouetting it against a stormy sky. Rollei SLX; 250 mm lens; 1/250 at f8; Ilford FP4.

113

Bird's-eye view

The majority of photographs are taken at a point somewhere between 4 and 6 feet (1½ and 2 metres) above ground level, because that is where a person of normal height usually holds a camera, and it is surprising how much interest and impact can be created in a picture by departing from this norm and taking a bird's-eye view of a subject. Even a small alteration in position can make a dramatic difference: most portraits, for instance, are taken with the camera approximately on a level with the model's eyes, and if you were to stand on a chair or sit your subject on the floor and shoot down, the result would automatically have a noticeably different visual quality. Even a still-life picture which is taken from above has a greater impact than one taken from a more conventional viewpoint. This is largely because such pictures have a more limited depth and perspective and the effect tends to produce a two-dimensional appearance with the emphasis directed more to the shape, colour, and texture of the subject, resulting in pictures with a more graphic quality.

This applies equally to the more obvious examples of this bird's-eye viewpoint such as a view from a hill-top or a high building, particularly when the camera is aimed directly down and especially when a long-focus lens is used. In these cases the result is often slightly unreal. The impression of height can be much more effectively created by the inclusion of foreground details such as the window from which a picture is taken; a wide-angle lens will emphasize this and increase the effect of perspective.

One of the problems frequently encountered with broad vistas from high viewpoints is atmospheric haze. In black and white pictures this can be largely overcome by the use of a red filter which eliminates the ultra-violet rays associated with haze; in colour a UV filter will have a limited but useful effect, and a polarizing filter will often help to reduce scattered light and increase the clarity of the picture. Ideally such pictures are best taken early or late in the day when the angle of light is more acute and the distant view is given a more bold relief.

Opposite below A fresh perspective can often be given to familiar sights by shooting from a high viewpoint. In this photograph of London a long-focus lens was used to isolate the Houses of Parliament from a small area of the scene. Nikon F3; 210 mm lens; 1/250 at f8; Ilford FP4.

Left The inclusion of foreground details has increased the impression of height in this shot taken from the Pompidou Centre in Paris; a wide-angle lens has emphasized the effect. Nikon F3; 28 mm lens; 1/125 at f8; Ilford FP4.

Left A high viewpoint has created a sense of order within a potentially confusing subject in this shot of a street festival. Nikon F; 50 mm lens; 1/30 at f2; Kodak Tri-X.

Photographic patterns

When a number of similar shapes are grouped together within a space a pattern is created. Even if the shapes are only superficially alike, provided they are spaced at regular intervals or are linked by lines of perspective or have a common tone or colour, the impression of a pattern is still produced. Patterns of this type can be found everywhere, in natural objects as well as in man-made structures, but in common with many of the other visual aspects of photography they can be all too often and too easily overlooked.

A pattern can be an invaluable aid to composition since it creates a sense of order and harmony within a picture and can add considerable impact. It is important to appreciate, however, that a pattern alone will not create a picture of lasting appeal, although it may have an initial and superficial stimulus on the viewer. It must be combined with other elements of composition such as colour, texture, and perspective.

Above The action of waves on sand has created a strong pattern which leads the eye naturally into the centre of the composition.

Right A series of pleasing shapes has been formed by this line of uniformed guardsmen.

A 'pure' pattern has no centre of interest and this is important in creating a pleasing and balanced image. Such is the visual force of a pattern that a disruption in the order of shapes or colours can become the focal point of a picture, with considerable effect, like one red apple in a box of green ones, for instance. The best approach is first to find your pattern and then to look for ways in which it can either be disrupted or juxtaposed against some contrasting element. Finding or creating a pattern is largely a question of viewpoint and framing; in this way a quite random arrangement of objects can be organized into an orderly and rhythmic image – the faces in a crowd, for instance – and often quite fleeting moments can create a pattern, such as a flock of birds.

Lighting can also have a marked effect and quite often something which has an inherent pattern, such as the leaves of a tree, may be more pronounced when lit quite softly while a hard directional light may create shadows which could confuse and disturb the regularity of the shapes. On the other hand, there are situations when a hard light with its interplay of shadows and highlights can actually be responsible for creating a pattern.

Left Patterns can be found everywhere as in this shot of the rows of tiles on a roof.

Below These carefully stacked pipes have produced a ready-made photographic pattern.

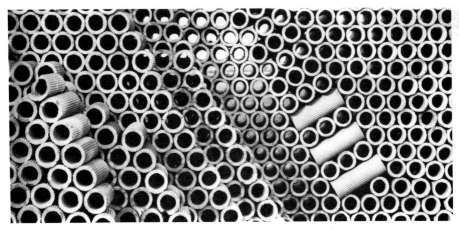

Using colour for mood

There is a very strong connection between colour and mood as reaction to colour is invariably emotive. The first step towards producing atmospheric and evocative colour photographs is an understanding of how and why we respond to colours in a certain way. The spectrum itself goes through a range of moods as well as colours: from the assertive qualities of red, for instance, with its connotations of warning and danger, to the warm and inviting moods of orange and yellow, the cool and restful attributes of green and blue, finishing with the rather sombre mood of indigo and violet.

In addition to the colour itself its hue or saturation will also affect mood; bright, fully saturated colours have a very vigorous, sometimes aggressive quality whereas soft pastel hues give a more gentle and romantic mood. The way that colours are mixed together in a picture will also have a considerable influence on the mood that is created. The presence of two or three contrasting colours, for instance, will create a lively and exciting atmosphere whereas a picture containing colours which blend and harmonize will produce a more relaxed and introspective mood.

It is vital to take all these things into consideration in order to create atmosphere in a picture. A lively, vigorous picture of children at play, for instance, would lose some of its effect if it consisted primarily of blues and greens whereas if it contained bold splashes of blue and red the liveliness of the subject would be emphasized. An excellent way of learning to control this aspect of picture-making is to set yourself the project of taking a series of pictures, each creating a different mood and making use of different colours and combinations. It would also be interesting to vary the subject, shooting perhaps a happy portrait, a sombre landscape, a restful still life, and so on. The experience you will gain from such an assignment will also help you with ideas for other projects such as illustrating a theme (pp. 164–5) or shooting a photo-essay (pp. 180–1).

Above left The warmth of the richly decorated interior of the Casino at Baden-Baden has been accentuated by shooting with daylight film. Pentax S1A; 28 mm lens; 1/2 at f11; Ektachrome 200.

Left The calm, quiet atmosphere of this Swiss lake scene has been given additional emphasis by the soft blue quality of the photograph shot on a dull overcast day. The natural blue bias of the light has been increased by the use of a blue colour correction filter. Nikon F3; 150 mm lens; 1/60 at f11; Ektachrome 64.

Above right The restful qualities of the colour green are exploited in this shot of trees on a Spanish hillside. The pattern of the trees adds to the mood. Nikon F2AS; 300 mm lens; 1/125 at f8; Ektachrome 64.

High-key photographs

Most photographs contain a full range of tones from the black of the deepest shadow to the white of the brightest highlight. Any image which departs radically from this arrangement derives its impact from this very difference. A high-key photograph is one where most of the image consists of tones from the lightest end of the grey scale with only a few darker tones to accentuate details. For this type of picture it is vital to have a subject which is essentially light in tone and has no bold contrasts or strong shadows.

In the studio with, say, a portrait or a still life it is of course possible to control both the tonal range of your subject and the background and also the lighting. A classic example of a high-key image would be a fair-skinned blonde girl wearing a white dress and placed in front of a white background with very soft frontal lighting that creates virtually no shadows.

Exposure is vital in this type of photography since a reading taken in the normal way will produce an image of grey tones instead of white. The best method of calculating exposure is either to take a reading from an 18 per cent grey card or to take an incident light reading; a reading taken directly from the subject will have to be increased by 2 to 3 stops. When shooting black and white or colour negative film it is in fact an advantage to over-expose slightly but with colour transparency film the exposure must be assessed precisely to avoid details being lost in the lightest tones.

In outdoor locations where you are unable to exercise such a fine degree of control over the lighting and the subject it is necessary to achieve your effect by the choice of viewpoint and the framing of the image so that dark tones are excluded and the lighting is soft and frontal. In these circumstances weather conditions such as snow, mist, or even rain can be exploited to achieve the desired result. Here again a degree of over-exposure can help to create the high-key quality but the most successful results will be produced with a very softly lit light-toned subject.

Right A large white tracing-paper screen close to the model was used to diffuse and soften the light in this portrait. A large white reflector was positioned near the model to prevent strong shadows being formed. Bare shoulders, a white background, and the model's blonde hair have completed the high-key effect. Nikon F; 105 mm lens; f11 with studio flash; Kodak Tri-X.

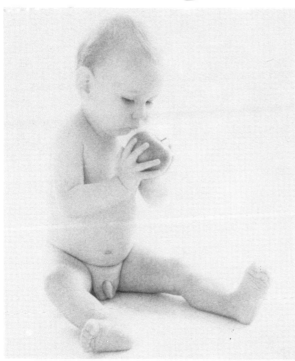

Left A studio flash was bounced from a white ceiling to light this baby sitting on a seamless white background paper. The absence of dark tones and shadows has produced the high-key effect. Nikon F2; 105 mm lens; f16 with studio flash; Kodak Tri-X.

Below left Shooting into the light, combined with a light-toned subject and slight overexposure, has produced this outdoor portrait. A small amount of flare caused by the sun shining on to the lens has also helped to soften the image. Rollei SLX; 150 mm lens; 1/125 at f5.6; Ilford FP4.

Below right A misty day which has created a virtually shadowless light and has masked background details has produced this light-toned image of a lone tree. Nikon F3; 200 mm lens; 1/60 at f8; Ilford FP4.

Creating a sense of touch

One of the qualities unique to the photographic process is its ability to reproduce the visual quality of a textured surface to a remarkable degree. Wood-grained textures, for example, are often reproduced on smooth plastic laminates so convincingly that you have actually to touch them to be sure that it is not the real thing. Even in a black and white photograph the tactile quality of an image can override the lack of colour and make the image seem 'real'. It is indeed a powerful element and when used appropriately can produce pictures with considerable impact and with great image quality.

The fundamental requirement is faultless technique: the lighting must be directed to create the optimum effect, the exposure must be calculated to reproduce the most subtle tones, and the image recorded to produce razor-sharp definition. It is no coincidence that the areas of professional photography which rely heavily on textural quality such as still life and food are dominated by

photographers who are first and foremost masters of technique and that the equipment they favour is invariably the large-format 8 × 10 view camera for the ultimate in image quality. Nevertheless images of equal impact can be produced with a 35 mm camera providing the necessary care is taken to exploit its capabilities to the full.

The first necessity is a suitable subject and the right lighting to emphasize its textural qualities. In the studio with a still life, for example, this can be achieved by manoeuvring the lights but outdoors the lighting must be controlled by the choice of viewpoint. As a general rule a fairly hard, acutely angled lighting is the most effective in revealing subtle textures such as skin, sand, or wood grain, but more pronounced textures require a softer, less directional light as otherwise large areas of dense shadow will be created and the subtleties of tones will be lost.

The image must be perfectly sharp and so a tripod should be used whenever possible, both to prevent camera shake and so that a

Left Shooting towards the light has caused it to glance off the slate-tiled roof, creating bold relief. Nikon F3; 200 mm lens; 1/125 at f8; Ilford FP4.

Above An acutely angled cross light has revealed the subtle texture of this Victorian ironwork. Nikon F3; 105 mm lens; 1/125 at f11; Ilford FP4.

small aperture can be used to obtain adequate depth of field. Exposure must be carefully estimated to ensure a full range of tones; the highlights are normally of greatest importance in this type of image and a degree of under-exposure will usually emphasize the textural effect whereas over-exposure will lessen it. To maximize the definition it is best to choose a slow, fine grain film such as Kodak Panatomic-X or Ilford Pan F with black and white pictures and Kodachrome 25 when shooting in colour.

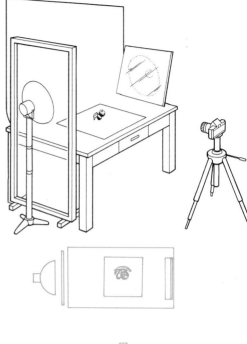

Above A soft but strongly directional light has emphasized the different textures of the fruit and the background. A small mirror placed close to the subject on the opposite side has relieved the shadows. The set-up is shown in the illustration (above right). Pentax 6 × 7; 150 mm lens; f16 with studio flash; Ilford FP4.

Right Late-afternoon sunlight across the body of this nude has produced a rich texture emphasized by an exposure calculated to give maximum detail in the highlights at the expense of the shadows. Rollei SLX; 150 mm lens; 1/125 at f11; Ilford FP4.

Worm's-eye view

Habit dictates a great many of our everyday activities and photography is no exception. One of these well-established habits is the position from which we take most of our pictures – a picture is seldom taken from ground level, for instance, and yet this simple change of viewpoint can make a significant difference to both the composition and the effect. It is not a very comfortable or convenient viewpoint, and indeed with an eye-level viewfinder it will invariably involve lying full length, and a camera with a waist-level viewfinder such as a twin-lens reflex is a distinct advantage. It is important to make allowance for exposure calculations with low-viewpoint shots outdoors since they will usually include a large area of sky; the meter should either be used close to the subject or angled down away from the sky for the reading.

The immediate effect of shooting from a low angle is in the perspective and unfamiliarity of the viewpoint. It will be much more apparent when the subject is quite close to the camera – a distant tree, for example, would show little change when viewed from normal height and ground level. The use of a wide-angle lens will also give considerable emphasis to the perspective effect when the camera is tilted upwards from ground level.

The mood of a picture will be affected by low-viewpoint shots; subjects will appear more dominant and assertive and will produce images with a more dramatic quality. An action shot of a high-jumper, for instance, will look more dynamic when shot from ground level. The shape of a subject will be given added emphasis, and shooting from a low viewpoint can be effective for creating silhouetted images and is often a good way of accentuating dramatic skies or sunsets with an interesting foreground. Animals and small children also frequently benefit from being photographed from their own level; in such cases do not forget that you can achieve the same effect by raising the subjects rather than by lowering the camera.

Right The graphic quality of this shot of a snow-covered tree has been emphasized by shooting directly upwards and isolating the branches against the sky, accentuating their shape and the pattern effect. Rollei SLX; 50 mm lens; 1/250 at f8; Kodak Tri-X.

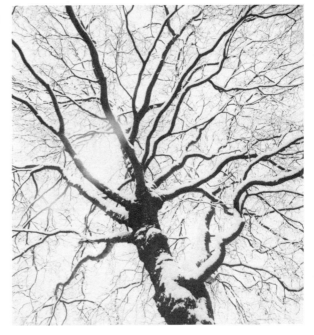

Above This dramatic view of the Eiffel Tower was shot from almost immediately underneath it with the camera aimed upwards. A wide-angle lens was used which has exaggerated the effect as well as permitting such a close viewpoint. Nikon F3; 20 mm lens; 1/125 at f11; Ilford FP4.

Left In this studio shot the worm's-eye viewpoint was produced by positioning the girl very carefully on a large plate-glass mirror and shooting down into it. Pentax 6 × 7; 105 mm lens; f11 with studio flash; Ilford FP4.

Keeping it simple

One of the main mistakes made by photographers, and one which is probably responsible for the majority of bad pictures, is putting too much into the frame. The single most important decision that a photographer has to make is what to include in the picture area. An element should only be included if it contributes to the meaning and composition of the picture. One of the most instructive ways of learning to isolate and select the elements of a picture is to keep the image as simple as possible; at the same time you will be able to produce photographs with a striking visual quality.

The most straightforward way of keeping the image simple is to move in close and frame the picture tightly so that almost everything but the main subject of the picture is excluded. This can be particularly effective with subjects such as portraits and animals where the emphasis is on expressions and gestures. Where for reasons of composition or simply for practicality more space is needed round the subject, it is very important to frame the picture in such a way that the subject clearly remains the focus of interest of the image.

The first step in achieving this is to ensure that there is a bold tonal or colour contrast between the subject and its surroundings. A dark-toned subject, for instance, should be juxtaposed against a background of a lighter tone and a brightly coloured subject placed against a neutral or contrasting hue. Secondly, the picture should be framed so that the subject is placed in the most dominant part of the image. This will depend to a degree on the other elements of the picture but you should consider your picture in terms of the way in which other objects relate to the main subject. If they compete for attention or create a distraction then you must either exclude them altogether or change your viewpoint so that they become subordinate to the main subject of the picture. On your next picture-making session try to see just how little you can include in the frame and still produce a meaningful image – you may be surprised!

Above Tight framing, an uncluttered background, and a bold contrast between subject and background have all contributed to the effect of this picture, adding impact to the slightly bizarre aspect of the subject. Nikon F3; 105 mm lens; 1/60 at f5.6; Kodachrome 64.

Right This picture relies on a composition based on the intersection of thirds as well as a boldly silhouetted subject and a restricted colour range, to create an image of almost stark simplicity. Nikon F3; 150 mm lens; 1/125 at f5.6; Ektachrome 64; polarizing filter to add depth to the colours.

Left The emphasis has been created here by placing the main subject of the picture at the intersection of thirds – a point where lines drawn one-third of the way along the sides of the picture meet. There is also a contrast of shapes as well as of colour. Nikon F3; 75 mm lens; 1/125 at f5.6; Ektachrome 64.

Low-key photographs

A low-key picture is one in which the majority of tones are at the dark end of the grey scale. The low-key effect can be created more successfully by lighting than can a high-key picture. A low-key image is an effective way of creating a feeling of mood and drama and of emphasizing texture. Using studio lighting with a portrait, for instance, the low-key effect can be produced by choosing a dark-toned background and clothes for the model and directing the main light sources from the side or even slightly behind the model rather than from the front.

It is important to avoid extremes of contrast, both within the subject itself and also with the lighting, since the essence of a low-key picture is a full range of dark tones which would be lost if the contrast were excessive.

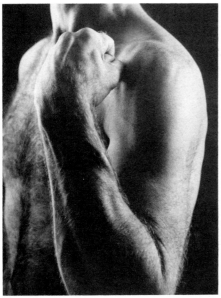

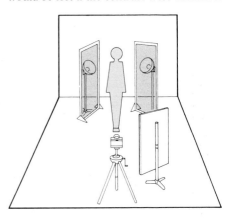

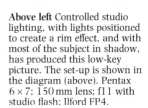

Above left Controlled studio lighting, with lights positioned to create a rim effect, and with most of the subject in shadow, has produced this low-key picture. The set-up is shown in the diagram (above). Pentax 6 × 7; 150 mm lens; f11 with studio flash: Ilford FP4.

Left The only highlights in this shot of a mountain road at dusk are created by the car headlights and the white line which have become the focus of attention. Nikon F2; 105 mm lens; 1/15 at f8; Kodak Tri-X.

128

It is important to realize that any highlights will become very dominant; their presence and position in the picture should be carefully considered as such areas will inevitably become the centre of interest of the image.

Exposure calculations must be made with care since a reading taken in the conventional way will produce an over-exposed result; a close-up reading from a medium tone is the safest method, or alternatively an over-all reading reduced by 2 to 3 stops. When shooting on negative film it is possible to produce a low-key effect at the printing stage, both by making the print darker and also by 'printing in' light areas. With colour transparency film, however, the effect must be created solely by the selection of the subject, the control of the lighting, and accurate exposure.

In outdoor situations the low-key effect is dependent on the lighting conditions, the weather, and the selection of viewpoint: with landscape pictures, for instance, stormy skies produce a rich range of darker tones, as will subjects lit by the low-angled light of late afternoon. Shooting into the light will in many cases also create the right conditions for a low-key picture.

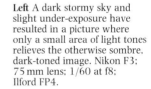

Above Shooting into the light has created an image with bright highlights; the low-key effect has been produced by exposing for the highlights and allowing the other tones to be under-exposed. Shooting from a different viewpoint with normal exposure would have produced a full range of tones and a normal image. Nikon F2: 24 mm lens; 1/125 at f11; Ilford FP4.

Left A dark stormy sky and slight under-exposure have resulted in a picture where only a small area of light tones relieves the otherwise sombre, dark-toned image. Nikon F3; 75 mm lens; 1/60 at f8; Ilford FP4.

Bold colour effects

A colour photograph is only ever effective if the colour has been used selectively and with discretion. The bright, multi-coloured scenes to which many inexperienced photographers respond most readily are unfortunately almost guaranteed to produce a disappointing result. A selective and limited use of colour does not mean, however, that it cannot be bold; in fact the less colour there is in an image the more impact will be created by what colour is present. The most dramatic effect will be produced by a picture which has a subject of a predominantly single colour set against a background of a contrasting colour or tone: for example, a red flower which is set against green foliage or against a black or white background.

A good way of learning the discipline required for a good colour picture is to give yourself a project to produce a series of pic-

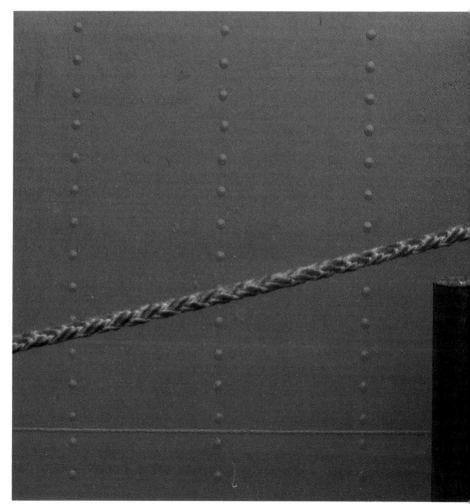

tures each representing one colour – red, green, blue, and yellow, for instance – so that even a quick glance at the picture will leave you with a strong impression of that colour. An added challenge is to see how small that tone can be while still being effective. The more saturated the colours, the greater the over-all impact will be.

Both lighting and exposure are important factors in enhancing the effect of a brightly coloured subject. As a general rule, a small degree of under-exposure will increase the colour saturation while over-exposure will weaken the colour. A soft light which creates only slight shadows is preferable as rich colours will be diminished by lighting which creates bright highlights and dense shadows – a slightly cloudy day or open shade is more suitable than bright sunlight. A polarizing filter can be an effective way of increasing colour saturation. Although this type of filter is most commonly used for highly reflective subjects such as glass you will find that the polarizing effect can often considerably reduce glare from foliage, flowers, blue skies, and painted surfaces.

Left This dockside detail shot depends for its impact on the dominance of the bright red hull and the spartan composition. Nikon F3; 105 mm lens; 1/60 at f8; Ektachrome 64.

Top The effectiveness of this shot results from the bold contrast between the two large areas of colour and the absence of any others. Nikon F3; 105 mm lens; 1/60 at f8; Orwochrome film.

Above A polarizing filter has been used to add depth and saturation to the colour of the sky, on which the success of this picture depends. Nikon F3; 105 mm lens; 1/60 at f8; Ektachrome 64; polarizing filter.

Shooting against the light

In the early days of photography a widely observed maxim was to keep the sun behind you when you were taking a picture. This was largely because of the limited speed and latitude of the film, but even with modern fast films which have a wide latitude the advice is still accepted as gospel and the great majority of photographs are taken with the sun behind the camera. This does ensure, however, that any picture taken into the sun has an immediate impact, but quite apart from its novelty value this technique has some other quite distinct advantages. For instance, it is an excellent way of isolating a subject from a cluttered or confusing background; a back-lit shot such as a portrait not only subdues background details but also often provides a halo of light around the edge of the subject, giving additional impact.

A common fault with such pictures is under-exposure because the meter is influenced by both the direct sunlight and the very bright highlights which are created. As a general rule, an increase in exposure of at least 2 stops will be required above that indicated by a meter used in the normal way,

but a much safer method, particularly with a portrait or similar subject, is to take a close-up reading, being especially careful to exclude both direct sunlight and highlights from the meter.

In addition to isolating a subject, back-lighting can also create a more dramatic effect. It invariably produces an increase in contrast, and by exposing for the lighter tones it is possible to create pictures with rich dark tones and luminous highlights, which is particularly effective with subjects that have a strong textural quality.

A problem that can arise is flare, which is an effect created by the indiscriminate scattering of light within the lens as a result of sunlight shining into it. Even with modern multi-coated lenses and the use of a lens hood it can still occur and as the result is drastically to reduce contrast it negates the effect of the lighting. This can usually be eliminated by shielding the lens with a piece of card or even your hand held at arm's length just outside the frame. This is only possible of course if the sun is not actually included in the frame, for which the camera must be 'hidden' within an area of shade. Wide-angle lenses are as a rule less prone to flare while you will find that most long-focus and zoom

lenses are very vulnerable.

In some circumstances, however, flare can produce a quite pleasing effect, creating images with a high-key quality and with pale pastel colours. A camera such as an SLR is required so that you will be able to judge the effect accurately.

Above left Including sun in the frame can create flare; here it is minimized by partially hiding the sun behind the tree. Nikon F3; 20 mm lens; 1/125 at f8; Ilford FP4.

Left Slight under-exposure has emphasized the textural quality. Nikon F3; 20 mm lens; 1/125 at f11; Ilford XP1.

Above right The shadow is dominant in the composition. Under-exposing has created a rich-toned, low-key image. Nikon F2AS; 28 mm lens; 1/125 at f8; Ilford FP4.

Right Back-lighting and exposing for the shaded face of the model have produced a picture with a plain white background. Rollei SLX; 150 mm lens; 1/125 at f8; Ilford FP4.

133

A picture story

The picture story was the main feature of the great picture magazines such as *Life*, *Look*, and *Paris Match*, and many of the great photographers who worked for these journals were masters of this aspect of the medium. The essence of a good picture story is that it combines the visual force of a series of individual pictures with the narrative power of the journalistic approach. In short, it uses pictures to describe a sequence of events in a logical and progressive way that needs only a minimal amount of text or caption material to complete the story.

The pictures must work in two ways, both as individual images each of equal interest and impact, and also as a series of images each linked to the next either thematically or chronologically. The challenge of achieving this is such that many of the legendary pictures by the great photographers have arisen

from a picture story sequence since this type of project makes a photographer really work at explaining, and fully understanding his subject and expressing this knowledge in purely visual terms. Although the picture story in this context has invariably been used to demonstrate events of world importance such as war and famine, the technique is just as challenging and effective when applied to more accessible situations such as a wedding or a family outing.

The key factor is good planning – you must know in advance as much about the occasion as possible; prepare a list of shots to establish the basic situation and the personalities involved and the climax of the event. You should try to cover all angles, more than you will need in fact since you will have to select and edit for the final sequence and it is far better to have a dozen shots too many than to find you lack one important picture. Aim to vary the types of picture, close-up and long-shot for instance, or wide-angle and telephoto, and also vary the tonal or colour quality and mood. All of these factors will help to create pace and excitement.

This series of pictures taken in a small Austrian village during the harvest establishes a number of facts about the event as well as conveying the atmosphere. They reveal that all the family lend a hand, from the youngest child to the oldest relative; the tools and method of working are shown, as is the village itself and the countryside in which it is situated. Pentax S1A; various lenses and exposures; Ilford FP4.

The wide-angle approach

One of the main advantages that has arisen from the development of the SLR camera is the wide and relatively inexpensive availability of a vast range of lenses of different focal lengths. Most photographers who have a camera that accepts interchangeable lenses soon acquire at least one lens in addition to the standard one with which the camera is fitted. The choice of a second lens is often difficult and will depend to a degree on the type of work which most interests you, but the main point is that whatever the choice, a lens of a different focal length can offer a completely new way of looking at a subject and a new way of approaching composition.

A wide-angle lens, for instance, has a lot more to offer than simply 'getting more in', although this is of course its most obvious effect and is the most basic reason for using one. In terms of composition, the effect on the perspective of an image is often the main contribution made by a wide-angle lens. The focal length of a lens does not alter the perspective of an image but it does enable you either to move closer to a foreground detail or to include a closer object without moving

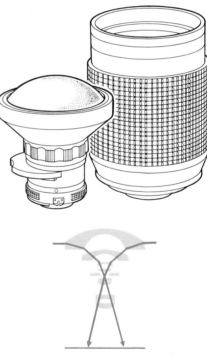

Above A 20 mm wide-angle lens was used to produce the strongly emphasized lines of perspective in this shot of Westminister. Nikon F3; 20 mm lens; 1/250 at f8; Ilford FP4.

The illustration shows a conventional wide-angle lens (top right) and a fish-eye lens (top left). The light-path diagram (below) indicates how the 180° field of view is achieved in a fish-eye lens.

further back; either way, the effect is a greater extreme of perspective. A 20 mm lens on a 35 mm camera, for instance, would enable you to include an object at only 1 foot or so (30 centimetres) in front of the camera as well as a distant scene; in addition, the depth of field is considerably greater than with a standard lens so that even at only a medium aperture of perhaps f8 both quite close and distant details can be recorded sharply. When this effect is used in a picture it produces strong images in which the impression of depth and distance is greatly enhanced, and it will also emphasize the lines of perspective which are created when objects or lines recede into the distance.

Another valuable aspect of wide-angle effects is the ability to approach a subject closely and at the same time to include a large area of a scene. This is often used in photo-journalism when photographing in crowded, active situations where the close viewpoint can help to create a more intimate and 'immediate' atmosphere, while at the same time the great depth of field makes focusing less critical. The main point when using a wide-angle lens is to avoid a confusing and jumbled image as a result of too much detail, and for this you should choose your viewpoint and frame the picture with care, while making sure that you have a boldly placed and clearly defined centre of interest.

Above The impression of depth and distance has been accentuated in this landscape by the wide-angle lens. The effect of the sky has also been increased. Nikon F3; 20 mm lens; 1/60 at f8; Ilford FP4; red filter.

Above right A close viewpoint has exaggerated the effect of perspective in this group portrait but the wide-angle lens enables all the faces to be included. Pentax 6 × 7; 55 mm lens; f11 with studio flash; Ilford FP4.

Right The 180° view of this picture is achieved by the use of a fish-eye lens. Its inherent circular distortion has lent itself well to this particular image. Nikon F3; 8 mm lens; 1/125 at f11; Ilford FP4.

137

Architectural details

The conventional approach to photographing a building is to include the whole structure in the picture, but there are other possibilities. One variation is to take a long shot that shows less detail of the building and more of its surroundings, which can in some ways be more informative and evocative. In a different way, a close-up picture which reveals individual details of a building, showing its method of construction for instance or the subtlety of texture or ornamentation that would be invisible from a more distant viewpoint, can be equally successful. In fact, a series of close-up images of a building can often say more about that building than one single photograph.

Where you can approach the subject quite closely and the details you want to photograph are no more than about 13 feet (4 metres) from the ground a standard lens will usually be quite satisfactory, but when a more distant viewpoint is necessary or the area of interest is at a higher level then you will need a long-focus lens.

Pictures of this type depend largely for their success on the use of bold elements of composition such as colour, texture, and pattern; the choice of viewpoint and the way in which the picture is framed are the main ways of ordering and controlling these elements. You should look for aspects of the building which enable you to juxtapose contrasting elements, one colour against another for instance, or the smooth quality of stone against the rough weathered texture of wooden beams. Try to frame the picture so that the shapes and lines within the image form a balanced whole.

Sometimes very small details such as ironwork or carvings can make strong pictures, but these must be of a very high technical quality if they are to be successful. Good definition is particularly vital for this type of work and since slow films and small apertures are usually required a firm tripod is an invaluable accessory; it also helps in framing the image precisely.

Lighting is another important factor as subtleties of form and texture are totally dependent on appropriate lighting. Hard, acutely angled lighting may well create harsh shadows which will lose the intricate details of a stonemason's work, for instance, but at the same time it may reveal the more subtle relief of textured wood or stone. Take careful account of both the quality and direction of the light when you are choosing your viewpoint.

Opposite above A long-focus lens has isolated a detail of this timbered clock-tower in a village in Alsace. Nikon F3: 150 mm lens: 1/125 at f8: Ektachrome 64.

Opposite below Strong sunlight has emphasized the texture of this weathered column in a bullring in southern Spain. Nikon F3: 105 mm lens: 1/250 at f8: Ektachrome 64.

Above Pattern is the feature of this picture of the Pompidou Centre in Paris. Canon F1: 100 mm lens: 1/125 at f16: Ektachrome 64.

Right Bold lines and colours predominate in this shot taken at the University of California. Hasselblad; 80 mm lens; 1/125 at f22; Ektachrome 200.

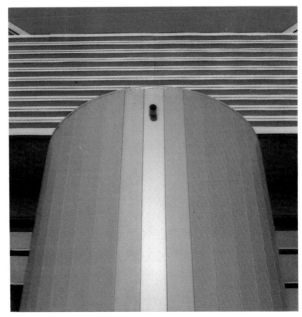

The telephoto approach

A telephoto or long-focus lens has a number of characteristics which are particularly useful to the photographer who likes to manipulate and control his images. The most basic of these is the ability to reach out optically and isolate a small area from a scene; this in itself can be a powerful creative tool since it can allow you to present an image removed from its original context, and in this way quite mysterious, even abstract, pictures can be produced from ordinary everyday situations. This is of course in addition to the more obvious convenience of the long-focus lens which produces a close-up image in a situation where you cannot approach closely enough, for example at a sports meeting.

The perspective effect of a long-focus lens is the opposite of that of a wide-angle lens since its narrow field of view limits the inclusion of close foreground details when shooting a distant scene and the effect of depth and distance is diminished. This produces pictures with a less three-dimensional quality and in which the scale of objects at different distances from the camera are seen closer to their true relative scales. When a very long lens is used and two or more objects are juxtaposed in this way the

Left A 600 mm mirror lens was used to take this shot of fishing enthusiasts on a pier. The camera was supported on a tripod. Nikon F2AS; 600 mm lens; 1/500 at f8; Kodak Tri-X

Right In this shot of a Kentish hop-field the compression of perspective was achieved by means of a 200 mm lens. Use of a tripod enabled a small aperture to be selected for adequate depth of field. Nikon F3; 200 mm lens; 1/15 at f16; Ilford FP4; orange filter.

effect can sometimes appear as a distortion of perspective but this is not actually the case; you are simply being presented with an unfamiliarly limited view of a scene. However, this juxtaposition of objects and comparison of scale can be used as a very effective element of composition in a photograph, and the flat two-dimensional effect can produce pictures with a bold sense of design, emphasizing shapes and lines and giving a strong graphic quality.

Long-focus lenses also have much shallower depth of field than standard or wide-angle lenses and this too can be used to good effect in terms of composition. Its main use is to enable you to create a bold separation between subject and background; even a fussy and confusing background can be reduced to a smooth soft tone by focusing accurately on the subject and using a fairly wide aperture. This can be very useful, for instance, when shooting portraits where you are unable to direct the model, such as candid shots in a busy street. Accurate focusing is vital as even at a distance of around 10 feet (3 metres) the depth of field will be very shallow when a wide aperture is used. Camera shake can be a problem with long lenses as they are also more difficult to hold steadily and a tripod or some form of support should be used whenever possible. As the image is in effect being magnified, a fast shutter speed should be selected; 1/250 sec is the minimum with lenses up to 200 mm.

Left The shallow depth of field of a long-focus lens used at a wide aperture has helped to isolate the man's face from a fussy background. Nikon F2AS; 200 mm lens; 1/250 at f4; Kodak Tri-X.

Nature in close-up

One of the major problems associated with the visualization of pictures is the ability to isolate details from a scene or a situation. Too often the eye is overwhelmed by the wider aspects of a subject, and this is particularly true of the natural world where many of the more beautiful and dramatic images are only revealed by a closer look. Close-up pictures are most easily taken with an SLR camera which can be fitted with either a bellows unit, extension tubes, or a macro lens so that the subject can be reproduced on the film at up to and even larger than life size. However, even a simple viewfinder camera can be used to take quite close-up pictures satisfactorily with an inexpensive close-up lens attachment, providing care is taken to line up the camera accurately, since at close focusing distances a viewfinder camera gives a false impression of the field of view because of parallax error. The actual centre of the picture can be found by holding a straight piece of wood along the lens axis when it will point at the centre of the image.

A tripod is an invaluable accessory for taking successful close-up pictures since it not only makes it easier to aim and frame the camera accurately but also helps to eliminate the possibility of camera shake. An inherent problem with close-up pictures is shallow depth of field; this decreases drastically at close focusing distances and in many instances a small aperture will be needed to produce a sharp over-all image of a subject. In other cases, however, the shallow depth of field can help to lift out and isolate a sharply focused subject from fussy and confusing surroundings.

Subject movement can be a problem in this type of photography, for example in the case of flowers where the slightest breeze will create vibration; this can be prevented by the use of a card screen or a thin piece of wood as a supporting splint. As well as the obvious colourful subjects like foliage and flowers, do not overlook the elements of pattern, texture, and form which are to be found in all objects in the natural world.

Right This picture of berries on a snow-covered bush was taken with the aid of an extension tube. It required only a small reduction in the minimum focusing distance of the normal camera lens and could just as easily have been taken with a supplementary lens on a simple camera. Nikon F3; 105 mm lens; 1/30 at f11; Ektachrome 64.

Left An almost 1:1 close-up of a section of an abelone shell has produced this abstract image. A macro lens was used to obtain the necessary image size, and the subject lit by daylight. Nikon F3; 105 mm macro lens; 1/4 at f16; Ektachrome 64.

Left The minimum focusing distance of a 50 mm lens was sufficient to obtain this shot of fungus and dead leaves. Such pictures are well within the capabilities of a simple camera. Nikon F3; 50 mm lens; 1/60 at f11; Ektachrome 64.

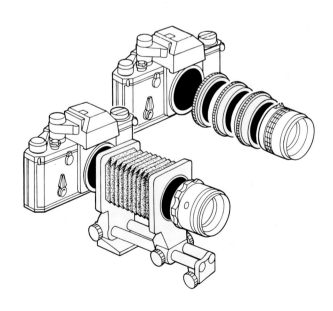

Above These two pictures show how the pattern and textural qualities of many natural objects can be emphasized and used to create effective images. They were photographed by the light of a window, with a white card reflector used to add detail to the shadows. Nikon F3; 105 mm lens with extension tube; 1/4 at f22; Ilford XP1.

Special Assignments

Dramatic skies

A photographer's ability to 'create' a dramatic sky is limited, for obvious reasons, but nevertheless some skill is needed to maximize the effect of such a sky when it does present itself as a potential subject. There are a few basic points to remember.

The main problem is exposure. The sky is a major part of the light source in most pictures and because of this an exposure which is adequate to create a full range of tones in the foreground of the scene will often result in over-exposure of the sky with a corresponding loss of density and tonal range. With black and white photography this can be overcome by simply 'printing in' the sky when the enlargements are made. This technique involves either cutting a mask to fit the shape of the horizon or using your hands to give additional exposure to the sky area alone.

When shooting colour transparencies it is necessary to achieve this effect in the camera. In many cases the best solution is to use a graduated filter: the square type such as the Cokin is the most convenient as it can be slid up and down in the mount so that the division between the clear and tinted plastic can be finely adjusted to fall along the horizon line – or wherever you want it. This technique can be an advantage even with black and white pictures as it avoids over-exposing the sky and the need to 'print in'. The neutral grey filter is the most useful one for emphasizing the natural moody effect of a stormy sky but the coloured range can also be effective if used with a little discretion – remember that too much colour can look unnatural unless you are shooting a sunset. It is important to make your exposure calculations before you fit the filter when using a TTL meter as you will otherwise have over-exposure which will negate the effect of the filter. Where you have a situation of blue sky and clouds a polarizing filter can be very effective when shooting in colour, or even a combination of a polarizing and a neutral graduated filter. With black and white film a red or orange filter will also give effective results where blue sky is present (pp. 46 – 7).

Another solution for both colour and black and white photography, particularly when you have a very dramatic sky, is to find a foreground subject which has an interesting or bold shape and to calculate the exposure for the sky, allowing the foreground to become silhouetted (pp. 112 – 13).

Below left A neutral-tone graduated filter combined with a degree of under-exposure has emphasized the rich tones of this grey sky. Nikon F3; 105 mm lens; 1/60 at f8; Kodachrome 64; graduated filter.

Right Shooting into the light and deliberately under-exposing by about 1 stop has produced the dramatic effect of the sky and its reflection in the water. Nikon F3; 150 mm lens; 1/250 at f11; Ektachrome 64.

Below A polarizing filter was used to darken the blue sky in this landscape, emphasizing the bold cloud formation. Nikon F3; 105 mm lens; 1/30 at f8; Kodachrome 25; polarizing filter.

147

Abstract nudes

People are the centre of interest of more photographs than any other subject and the variety of style and approach which photographers adopt is enormous. In the great majority of these pictures it is the identity of the person which is important or what he or she is doing or represents. The human body is, however, an ideal subject for those who are more interested in images in which composition, lighting, texture, and form are sufficient justification for a picture rather than the desire to create a representation of a person or an object.

The abstract nude has long been a popular subject for photographers who are interested in the medium as a means of self-expression and wish to produce work of a more personal or interpretative nature, but in addition to this, photographing the nude is an excellent

way of learning the technical aspects of photography.

While it is quite possible to produce such pictures using daylight a greater range of controls and variety of effects are possible when studio lighting is used. This need by no means be complex – two or three photofloods on stands, combined with a diffusing screen and a reflector, can be quite adequate, since only a quite small area is being lit and even with colour or slow black and white film the exposures will be quite practicable.

Backgrounds can also be quite modest. In most cases a plain wall will be adequate and a variety of tones can be introduced by lighting; when working in colour and when greater variety is needed, rolls of coloured background paper can be obtained from professional photographic stores.

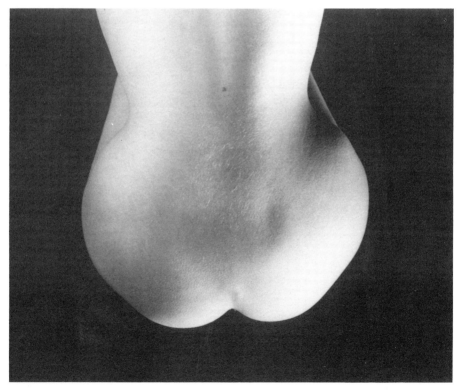

Finding a suitable model is much less of a problem than in conventional glamour work since the photographer is not concerned with conforming to the popular concepts of male or female beauty. The impersonal nature of the pictures is also likely to be less inhibiting to friends who might otherwise feel vulnerable in front of the camera. Do, however, be careful about the appearance of the skin. This type of picture often requires lighting which emphasizes skin texture but at the same time it will accentuate blemishes and the marks left by clothing; do not hesitate to ask your model to use a little make-up if necessary to avoid such problems.

The pleasure of this type of session lies very much in the ability to experiment with lighting effects, the choice of viewpoint, and the way in which the image is composed and framed, and in doing so you will greatly extend your experience of both the technical and aesthetic aspects of photography.

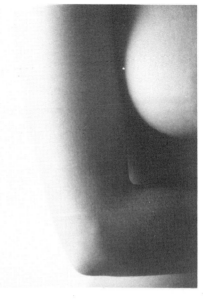

Left An unfamiliar viewpoint and tight framing have combined to create this bold, simple shape. Pentax 6 × 7; 105 mm lens; f16 with studio flash; Ilford FP4.

Above right A soft but strongly directional light has produced quite pronounced shadows and emphasized the shape of the model's body as well as introducing a degree of abstraction. Nikon F3; 105 mm lens; f11 with studio flash; Ilford FP4.

Right The lighting has been used to create an almost silhouetted image in this shot which emphasizes the lines of the model's body. Rollei SLX; 150 mm lens; f11 with studio flash; Ilford FP4.

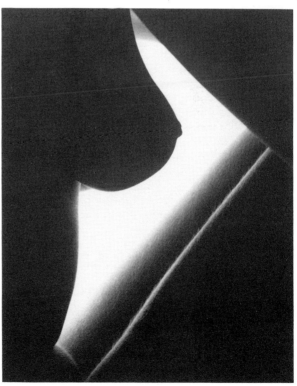

Instant art

Instant picture film is largely regarded as a snapshot medium or at best a means of trying out ideas or checking a set-up before using conventional film. An increasing number of photographers are discovering, however, that the qualities of the instant picture film lend themselves well to more creative use. The most obvious of these qualities is of course the ability to see the result within minutes of shooting the picture. This is helpful if you are producing images where individual pictures relate to each other, when an instant picture is incorporated into the subject and re-photographed for example; or if you are planning a mosaic of images, in which case each image can be assessed instantly in terms of its effectiveness with the pictures that have already been taken and any necessary adjustments made to the density, composition, or colour quality.

In addition to the immediacy of the image there are other ways in which it can be manipulated. This depends on the film type being used, and one of the most effective types of manipulation only works on the Polaroid SX–70 film, namely firmly massaging the surface of the film with a smooth blunt tool such as the end of a pen. If this is done during the period in which the image is forming, the dyes can be loosened and moved around under the surface of the film causing them to intermix, producing results ranging from subtle textural effects to wild distorted swirls of colour. After the image has formed it is also possible to cut away the back of an SX–70 print with a craft knife and to add colour dyes with a brush to the exposed image; you should wear rubber gloves when doing this to avoid contact with the caustic chemicals.

Peel-apart film can also be manipulated by scoring the film sandwich as it is processing; the processed print can also be soaked in hot water and the emulsion stripped away and transferred to another acetate support which then allows stretching and distortion to be carried out with ease.

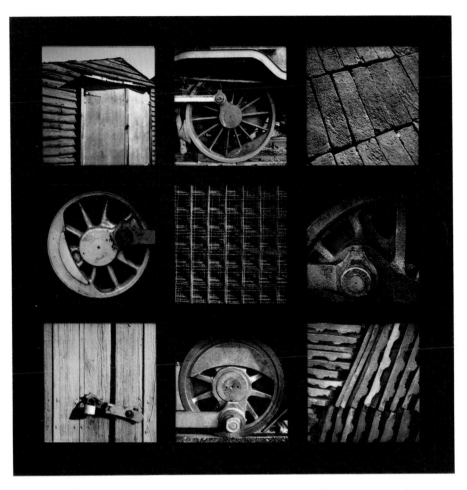

Far left This effect was produced by massaging the surface of an SX–70 print with a knitting needle during processing. Polaroid SX–70.

Left This picture uses the immediacy of the instant print camera to enable a photograph of the fruit shot on a plain background to be substituted in the final arrangement without the need for delay. Polaroid SX-70.

Above This picture shows how a series of instant prints can be used to create a mosaic where each image is shot so that its relationship to the others in the composite can be assessed immediately. Polaroid SX–70.

151

Shooting a picture series

Although the aim of most photographers is to produce individual pictures, each telling its own story or expressing a particular idea, it can be an interesting and challenging variation to take a series of pictures, each one of which is an individual element in a composite image. There are a number of ways in which this approach can be applied. One approach is to take a series of pictures of the same location or situation in which a different activity or a period of time creates a bond between the images; this could be done chronologically so that the individual photographs create a narrative, unfolding a plot or depicting a logical sequence of events. Alternatively, you could deliberately make no attempt to link the pictures in a way that invites the viewer to follow a story line, and instead create an impression where the connection between the pictures is only implied by some common element, leaving the viewer to interpret the sequence in his own way.

Whatever effect the sequence is intended to have, the important thing is to visualize the final result and to plan the individual pictures accordingly; you must decide how the sequence will be presented, whether as a series of images like the pages of a book or as a composite mounted together and viewed simultaneously. There are many ways in which the pictures could be linked: by shape, where a number of different subjects each has a circular motive perhaps, or by colour where, for example, each image progresses through the colours of the rainbow.

There is no reason why such a sequence cannot have a quite practical application, perhaps explaining how something is made. It might, for example, be an enjoyable exercise to produce a sequence of pictures depicting the letters of the alphabet for a young child which could be effectively made into a picture wall in the child's bedroom.

Left The element of continuity in this sequence was provided by photographing a number of different people in the same situation – looking out of a bus window. Although taken over a period of time and at different locations, and of course of different buses, the similarities in framing and setting form a common link, emphasizing the expressions and reactions of the captive subjects. Nikon F3; 150 mm lens; various exposures; Ilford XP1.

Sunsets

Most photographers find a sunset an almost irresistible subject as the rich tones and colours which it can provide are key factors in the production of a high-quality photographic image. It is true to say, however, that a very high proportion of the film expended on sunsets produces dull and disappointing results. The most common reasons for this are that the exposure has been miscalculated or that the picture lacks other interest.

·In order to reproduce the tonal richness of a sunset it is vital to avoid over-exposure, and indeed a degree of under-exposure will do much to increase the dramatic quality of a scene. A good rule of thumb for calculating exposure is to take a reading from the area of sky immediately above the camera, but when shooting a sunset it is always advisable to bracket the exposures quite widely, even to 2 stops each side, as the effect will vary enormously and it is difficult to predict the best result with any accuracy.

The problem with this type of picture is that the sunset itself is the brightest part of the image, which means that any under-exposure will record the other darker details such as the foreground without tone or detail. One way to overcome this is to select a viewpoint which enables you to use a foreground detail which has an interesting shape or outline, such as a tree, and which can be allowed to become silhouetted without losing its interest. Another solution is to find a foreground which is reflective, an expanse of water or even a wet street for example, since this will make it possible to

continue the tones and colours in the sky into the foreground.

A third solution is to use a graduated filter which enables a reduced exposure to be given to the sky area but at the same time leaves the foreground area normally exposed. This is simply a clear glass or plastic attachment of which only half is tinted so that it can be adjusted to coincide with the horizon line of the image. The filters are available in two strengths and in a variety of colours as well as neutral grey and can be used in combination.

The effect of most sunsets can be enhanced by the use of, say, a mauve- or tobacco-coloured filter and even a rather weak sunset can be made to record with rich, dramatic tones if a colour filter is used with discretion. Care should be taken to avoid over-filtration as the effect will appear artificial if the technique is allowed to become obtrusive.

Left This shot of the Negev Desert, taken shortly after the sun had gone down, has a rather soft, monochromatic quality. Nikon F; 200 mm lens; 1/60 at f5.6; Ektachrome 64.

Above A bold and interesting shape has been used to add to the composition of this picture. Nikon F2AS; 105 mm lens; 1/125 at f5.6; Ektachrome ISO 200/24°.

Above These four pictures illustrate the effect of different exposures on the quality of the image; they show a 2-stop bracket in ½-stop stages. Nikon F3; 105 mm lens; 1/60 at f5.6 to f11; Ektachrome ISO 200/24°; neutral graduated filter.

A contact sheet mosaic

This technique requires some care and more than a little patience, but is an effective and unusual way of presenting an image and is not difficult to do if carried out methodically. The main requirement is a firm tripod with a pan and tilt head, preferably one which is calibrated. The technique can be used with either roll film or 35 mm cameras and in colour or black and white but it is important if the processing is done by someone else that you ask for the film to be returned uncut. It is also preferable to use a long-focus lens; 135 mm on 35 mm cameras is ideal.

If you use a 135 mm lens to make a 36-exposure mosaic for contact-printing on to a sheet of 8×10 paper, it will in effect produce a picture with approximately a 120° field of view, so you must choose your subject with this in mind. With the camera mounted on a tripod, make sure that it is perfectly level so that the horizon stays in the same position when the camera is panned from one side of the scene to the other; a spirit level is a useful accessory for checking this position.

The most effective way of planning a sequence of shots is to use the calibrations on the pan and tilt head to ensure that each of the movements between shots is uniform. This can be done visually but is difficult especially in areas where there is little detail, such as sky. It is vital that the sequence of exposures is made in the same direction that the film travels in the camera, for example from left to right with the majority of 35 mm cameras, and from top to bottom with most roll film cameras. To produce a realistic effect the exposure should be averaged for the entire scene and not altered for individual frames, though it is of course possible to alter exposures on occasional frames to create a more interesting effect.

When shooting in colour, occasional

frames can be filtered to produce, say, a blue or red frame in selected parts of the image. Another variation is to shoot an occasional frame completely out of sequence or even to shoot a different subject. Since with a full 35 mm contact sheet you will use 36 frames it is advisable to load and unload the camera in very subdued light to eliminate the possibility of losing a vital frame through fogging. It is not essential to use all 36 exposures at once and for a first attempt it would be easier to attempt a more modest mosaic with

perhaps 4 frames along and 3 frames down, although the resulting contact print will of course be smaller.

Special requirements

A tripod with a calibrated pan and tilt head

A spirit level

A long-focus lens

The illustration on the right shows the sequence of pictures required to produce the mosaic on the opposite page. In this case the film went from top to bottom of the camera, and the shooting sequence follows this order. With a camera where the film went from left to right the final sequence would run horizontally rather than vertically, as shown in the illustration below right. This is the way it would have to be done with a 35 mm camera in the horizontal position. Rollei SLX; 150 mm lens; 1/60 at f8; Ilford FP4.

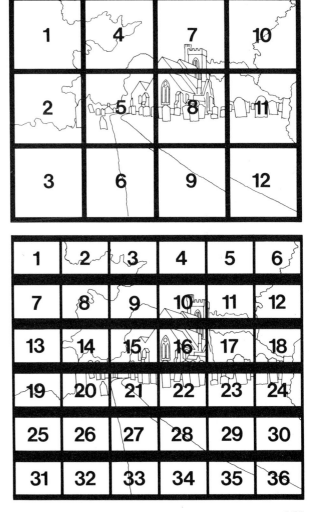

Making a flick book

Making a flick book is a way of creating the effect of movement using a sequence of pictures of a piece of action. It involves making small prints of the pictures which can be bound together and flicked with the thumb to create a smooth continuous action. A considerable number of prints (at least 50) are needed to produce a reasonable length of action but as the prints do not have to be very large it is possible to produce them as contact prints. For this you will need at least $2\frac{1}{4}$ inch square negatives which should be printed leaving spare paper along the top or side edge of the picture to allow for binding.

To take the pictures you should mount your camera on a tripod so that the framing remains totally static throughout the sequence. Your subject should be boldly defined against a contrasting background and the movement or action should be one that enables the model's limbs to be well displayed. It should also be something which can be done in slow motion since even with a motor drive with five frames a second a normal action will appear too fast when flicked.

It is best to make the prints on a resin-coated paper as this is more springy than a fibre-based paper and is less likely to become marked or permanently bent. Before cutting up the prints, or if making them individually, it is best to number them sequentially as they may be difficult to place in order when separated. The prints can be bound together by gluing the binding edge and clamping them together firmly until dry, or with a small sequence a very large clip may be adequate. Another method is to punch holes in the prints with a two-pin punch and then fasten and clamp them together with the devices used in box files or ring binders.

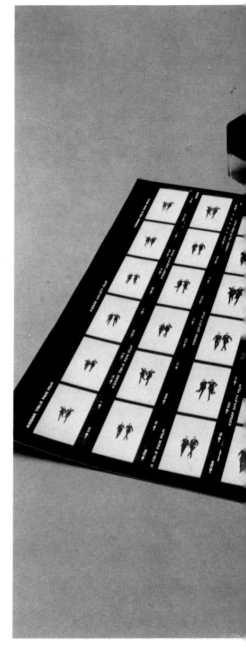

Right The picture shows the elements needed to make a flick book: the sheet of contact prints, two numbered prints, a magnifying glass and marker pencil, and the finished flick book.

Above These are two of the various methods of fastening the prints in a flick book: (top) by means of a plastic clip which is slipped on to hold the prints together at the edge; (bottom) here, holes have been punched through the prints which are held between two pieces of card, secured by two nuts and bolts.

A panoramic photograph

Even with an ultra wide-angle lens the maximum field of view that can be included without considerable distortion is about 110°. There is, however, an effective way of producing a wide-angle view of a subject up to 360° with even a simple camera and with no distortion. The method is to take a series of pictures traversing the scene and to cut and join the prints to produce a continuous image. It is vital to use a tripod and to ensure that the camera is perfectly level before the exposures are made; this can be checked with a spirit level.

Once you have established the outer limits of your picture you should make a 'dry run' with the camera, noting how many images will be required. It is important to allow a generous overlap at the edge of each frame, up to 25 per cent, which will make cutting and joining easier and will also minimize any perspective distortion which may be created at the edges of the frames. For this reason it is best to use a standard or even long-focus lens even though more images will be required to traverse the scene. Although it is possible to shoot a panorama on a wide-angle

lens more care is needed to choose the join-line and to ensure that the camera is level.

Remember to use the same exposure for each image; this can be estimated by taking an average from the lightest and darkest areas of the scene. The same applies if you are making your own prints – make a good print from the most representative negative and print the others exactly the same.

For joining the prints you will need a sharp razor blade or model tool, a steel straight edge, and a mounting-board and mounting adhesive. When making the cuts choose a line at which there is a minimum of detail or a natural vertical line in the scene; any slight inadequacies in the joining can be disguised by means of carefully retouching and re-photographing the finished composite. Simpler variations which require less care in alignment and cutting include making the sequence of exposures in the same way as the contact sheet mosaic (pp.156–7) and making a contact print or enlargement from the uncut strip of negatives. Another method is to shoot and print the sequence of images separately and to frame and mount them on a wall.

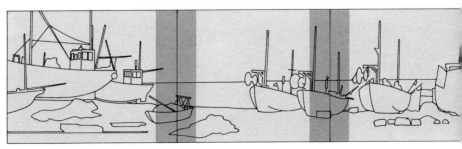

In each case the illustration shows the number of pictures required and the degree of overlap that was allowed to create the adjoining composite image. The vertical shot was made by lining the camera up on a central detail and keeping this in the centre of the viewfinder as the camera traversed the scene. The horizontal image was lined up using the horizon as a stabilizing line. In both cases the exposure was calculated by taking the average reading, and the same exposure given to each individual picture; the same principle was applied to making the prints. (Below left) Nikon F3; 75 mm lens; 1/125 at f8; Ilford FP4. (Left) Nikon F3; 105 mm lens; 1/250 at f8; Ilford FP4.

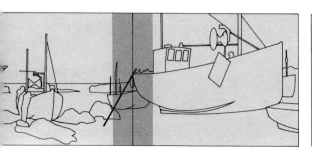

Shooting a step-by-step sequence

One of the advantages of photography is that it has brought a powerful and effective new element to education in that it can actually show how things are done, by recording the individual steps in a process of construction, for instance, or a progression of movements. To shoot a sequence in this way can provide both a challenging and instructional project and also a useful end-result. Your approach will to a degree depend on the process you are illustrating; in some instances it may be best to shoot the pictures over the head of the demonstrator (this is usually most effective where careful hand-work is involved such as pottery or metal-craft).

It is of course vital that every detail should be clearly seen: choose a plain contrasting background and fairly soft frontal lighting so

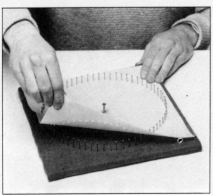

Above This series of pictures shows the main stages in the construction of a string sculpture, and only a few words of caption would be needed to supplement the visual information contained in the sequence. Soft overhead lighting was used to minimize shadows and make all details visible. The pictures were taken from the same viewpoint to give a feeling of continuity. Nikon F2; 105 mm lens; f16 with studio flash; Ilford FP4.

that important details are not lost in shadow, but remember that it is important to retain good modelling and texture. It is best to ask the demonstrator to do a trial run first so that you have a clear idea of the process and can establish the most salient points and select the most effective angles. It is also a good idea to take an establishing shot to show the basic set-up before work commences, and if appropriate a still-life arrangement of ingredients or tools. Both long shots and close-up pictures are often needed of the same stage to show the over-all effect of an operation and its individual detail and function.

In some cases you will need to indicate the scale of an object, and this can usually be achieved by including a hand in the picture. Where possible it is best to keep to the same viewpoint to maintain continuity, but this should not be done at the cost of visual information; if necessary, two views can be taken of a particular stage, one from the established viewpoint to retain continuity and another from the more revealing angle.

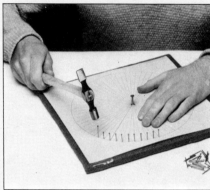

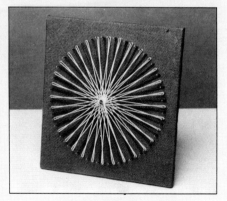

Illustrative photography

Most pictures taken by amateur photographers are the result of a spontaneous reaction to a scene or situation, and this is indeed a satisfying way of producing photographs. The majority of professional photographers, however, work to a brief based on an idea which has been thought out and visualized by a client or designer to promote a product or service. This approach to photography can be both challenging and instructive for an amateur since it stimulates the imagination and encourages the development of technical expertise in order to realize the visual idea. The method is frequently used as a means of instruction in art colleges and photographic schools for this reason and the motivation is provided by an end-product which may be anything from a record sleeve to a poster.

Above Translating the mood or quality of a piece of music into purely visual terms is of necessity very subjective, but also a stimulating challenge. This 'disturbed landscape' had something of the feeling of Mahler's music for both the photographer and the record company. Nikon F; 105 mm lens; 1/4 at f16 with controlled camera shake; Ektachrome 64 (colour original).

Left This picture was taken to illustrate a feature to be published in a 'girlie' magazine on the involvement of the Mafia in the night-life and vice centres of large cities. Hasselblad; 150 mm lens; f11 with studio flash; Ilford FP4.

Right The brief for this shot was an illustration of a short story set in the future where people may have themselves put into cold storage and be revived at a chosen time. An aerosol can of Christmas frosting was the crucial prop. Hasselblad; 150 mm lens; f8 with studio flash; Ilford FP4.

The best way to begin such a project is to imagine that you have been commissioned by a client to produce a photograph to be used in an advertisement, poster, or book jacket. It helps to give yourself precise specifications, and an unusual or unfamiliar subject will also help to stimulate your imagination. If you have friends who are also interested in photography it can be a good idea to set each other projects, or to take it in turns to set a project which you all attempt and to compare results. This will be an added

incentive to avoid the obvious and to find a more unusual solution.

Take the time to do some research for it invariably produces both a more eye-catching idea and a less obvious solution. It is a good idea to look at advertisements to see how other people have visualized pictures and overcome problems, and to decide if you can find a better or more interesting solution. Another possibility is to apply your visualizing abilities to more practical ends such as personal greetings cards (pp. 166 – 7).

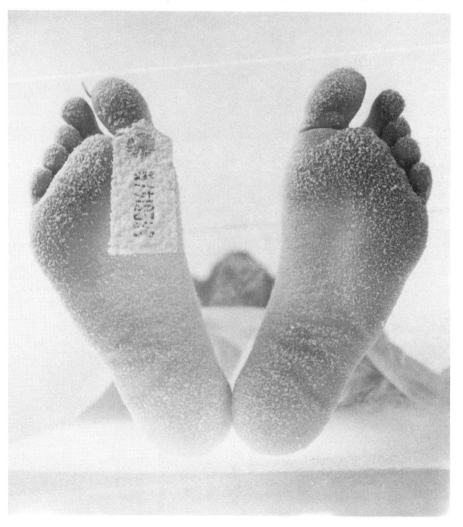

Making calendars and greetings cards

In most cases when an amateur photographer takes a picture it is an end result in itself to be mounted in an album or hung on a wall. Many professional photographers, however, produce images which are going to be incorporated with other elements of graphic design to become, say, an advertisement, a poster, or a brochure. There is no reason why the enthusiastic amateur should not both plan and use his pictures with a wider application in mind; one possibility is to make personal greetings cards, invitations, and calendars. An added bonus is that other design considerations such as lettering will help to make you more conscious of the graphic qualities of your photographic images.

The main consideration is the way in which the photographic image can be combined with the lettering. If the message is simple and you are making only two or three copies – a poster, for instance – the most

straightforward method is to use instant press-down lettering which can be applied directly on to the surface of the photograph. However, when larger numbers of copies and complex messages are involved other means must be found.

One method which can look very professional is to make up a piece of artwork using instant print and to have this printed professionally on to cards with the message in the correct position. The photographs can then be positioned and dry-mounted directly on to the printed card. Another method which gives a well-finished result is to make a copy negative of the artwork lettering and to print this directly on to the photographs using the montage printing technique described on pages 190–1.

If you are making a greetings card from colour prints it may be possible to incorporate the lettering on the transparency by using the double exposure technique

(pp.36–7) or by making a slide sandwich (pp.204–5). If you are shooting a picture specially for the design you may be able to include the message within the image: an invitation to a children's party, for instance, could be lettered directly on to an inflated balloon which could then be incorporated into the photograph.

Do not allow things to become too complex – the most effective designs are invariably the most simple and direct. Think of a good strong idea to begin with, preferably something with a particular touch of wit, humour, or drama according to the occasion; it can in fact be as much fun simply thinking of a good idea as actually carrying it through.

Left This Christmas card was made by mounting a print on a pre-printed card. The same effect could have been produced by lettering directly on to the photograph and then copying it, or by photographing the lettering and then double-printing it on

to the photograph by the method used in montage printing (pp.190–1).

Above The lettering in this calendar illustration was combined by first copying it on to Lith film and then projecting it on to the bottle in the still-life arrangement in the method described in projector effects (pp.16–17).

167

Using simple optics

Modern camera lenses are capable of recording extremely fine detail with great clarity, and for most pictures this is what is required. There are instances, however, where less definition and clarity can be an advantage, by creating a softer or more atmospheric image. Much of the attraction of the early Victorian pictures is dependent on the mellow, luminous quality which their simple lenses produced.

The most basic device is the pinhole and as well as being fun to make and use, it can also produce quite striking images. The best way of making a pinhole is to pierce a piece of aluminium foil with a fine needle and to tape this over the camera aperture. While it is possible simply to replace the lens of your SLR with the pinhole it can also be fun to construct a camera. Any light-tight container will do as long as the interior is painted matt black and you can fix a piece of film into one end. In a large box you could try using printing paper – a sheet of 8×10 bromide, for example – to produce a paper negative from which you can make a contact positive, or if you make your own colour prints you could try a sheet of reversal paper such as Cibach-

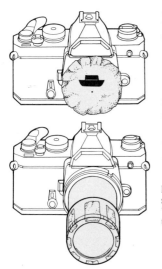

Above left This pinhole camera has been made by taping a piece of aluminium foil with the pinhole on to the body of an SLR.

Below left The magnifying-glass lens used to take the picture opposite was mounted on the camera by means of cardboard tubes.

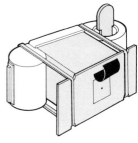

Above right A small cardboard box with the pinhole was taped on to a film cartridge to make a simple camera.

Below right The illustration shows the construction of the 'biscuit tin' pinhole camera used to take the picture above.

rome. This method of course allows you only one shot before returning to the darkroom to reload. An alternative is to construct a small box which fits directly on to a film cartridge or a Polaroid back.

A pinhole does not need to be focused which means that you can alter the angle of view by simply adjusting the distance between the pinhole and the film. When this equals the diagonal of the film it will produce a 'normal angle' of about 45°; a shorter distance will produce a wide-angle effect and a longer distance a telephoto effect. Exposure must be by trial and error since there are

many factors involved, but the average pinhole will require an exposure of something in the order of 1000 times that of a camera lens at f8. Once you have established a factor you can use your exposure meter in the normal way and multiply the reading by the factor.

In addition to pinholes there is considerable potential in experimenting with simple lenses such as magnifying glasses, Fresnel lenses, and even old box-camera lenses which can be mounted on to an SLR with cardboard tubes. The effect is often more pleasing than that produced by using soft focus devices with a high definition lens.

Right This soft focus nude was produced by mounting the lens from a magnifying glass on a single-lens reflex by means of a cardboard tube and adhesive tape. Pentax 6 × 7; approx. 120 mm lens (aperture approx. f2.2); 1/250 at f2.2; Ektachrome 200 (colour original).

Left This photograph was produced in a pinhole camera made from a large biscuit tin. The negative was made on a piece of bromide paper approx. 5 × 10 in and required an exposure of 3 minutes in bright sunlight. The final image was made by contact-printing the paper negative on to another sheet of bromide paper.

Right These two diagrams show the effect on the angle of view created by moving the pinhole closer to or further from the film.

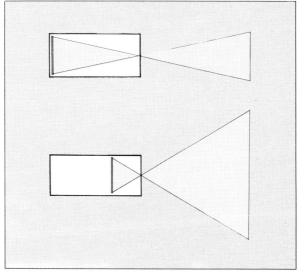

Physiograms

This is a simple and entertaining project, but one that can yield images with an original and exciting appeal. Physiograms can be photographed successfully in black and white but the most dramatic and exciting results are obtained with colour film. The main requirements are a room that can be completely darkened, a camera that can make time exposures, a firm tripod, a large mirror, and a flashlight with some string, together with coloured acetates or filters.

The basic principle is to make a time exposure of the path which the flashlight, suspended from the ceiling, traces as it swings in a series of loops or circles. The room should be completely dark and care taken that stray light is not reflected from the flashlight.The camera should be aimed from immediately below the light as it hangs in a static position; by using the mirror it is possible to position

the camera in a comfortable and convenient way (see diagram).

The colour can be introduced by placing a colour filter over the light or over the camera lens. The second method enables the filter to be changed during the exposure so that variation of colour can be introduced without interrupting the trajectory of the flashlight. The pattern which is created can be controlled by the way in which the light is swung and by placing a lens cap on the camera at the end of one trajectory, and two or more patterns can be combined on the same frame.

Exposure will be dependent on the intensity of the light, and it is best to use tungsten colour film; with a film of 160 ASA and a

The diagram shows the set-up of the lights and camera for both a simple and a more intricate physiogram.

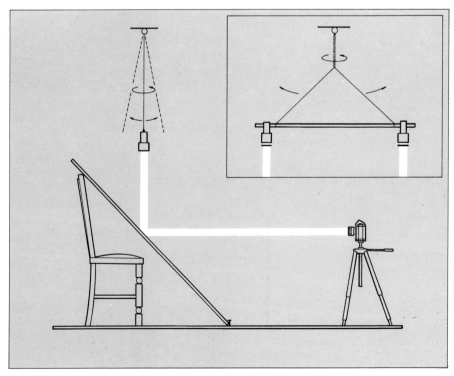

normal hand flashlight the aperture required will probably be about f11, though this will of course depend on the density of the colour filters. The actual length of the exposure will not affect the density of the image on the film but simply control the size and complexity of the pattern.

There are many variations which can be introduced to add further interest; instead of an actual flashlight, two or three flashlight bulbs can be mounted along a piece of wood and this in turn can be suspended from each end and wound up like the propeller of a toy aeroplane so that the bulbs will then rotate around each other as the wood unwinds as well as being swung into an elliptical trajectory. Attachments such as star-burst filters, diffraction gratings, and even multiprisms can be used to create more intricate effects. As well as being pleasing images in their own right, physiograms are ideal for combining with other images, by projection or double exposure, for example.

Special requirements

A darkened room

A tripod

A camera with a time exposure capability

A mirror

A flashlight or bulbs and batteries

String

Colour filters

Above Three trajectories were exposed on to one piece of film, with a different-coloured filter for each.

Above right Two bulbs, each covered by a colour filter, were fitted on a piece of wood which rotated like a propeller.

Right Here, a diffraction grating was fitted over the camera lens. Pentax 6 × 7; 105 mm lens; Ektachrome tungsten film.

171

A print portfolio

Good presentation is a vital aspect of photography as a good picture poorly presented will lose much of its impact, and a well-planned and well-prepared portfolio is an ideal showcase for your work. In addition, the process of putting a portfolio together will give you extra stimulus and satisfaction in the accomplishment of your projects.

There are essentially two types of presentation; the first is an album type in which the photographs are displayed on leaves which can be attached to a ring binder which permits easy removal. The albums are available with acetate sleeves which protect the surface of the prints, or the prints can be mounted on to boards which can be punched with holes to fit the ring binder. Even if the prints are displayed in the acetate sleeves they will look better and more finished if they are first mounted on to card. Dry mounting is best as it produces a smooth flat finish but spray mountants can be effective if used carefully, especially with resin-coated papers which are naturally quite smooth and flat. An alter-native is to have the pictures laminated; this involves encapsulating them in a film of clear plastic which gives both protection and rigidity, but does lose some of the image quality of an uncovered print surface.

The second method of presentation is a portfolio box. This is ideal if you are making prints for exhibition or display as the individual pictures can be mounted to create the best effect for each image and they do not have to be a uniform size or shape. Some photographers prefer to tape their prints to mounting boards and use a matt overlay in preference to the more permanent mounting techniques. However, this type of presentation is not as suitable for pictures designed for promotional or sales use where they are liable to damage from frequent handling.

The most important thing in any form of print presentation is the removal of dust marks and blemishes by spotting and retouching; nothing creates such a bad impression as a marked or blemished print no matter how well mounted and displayed.

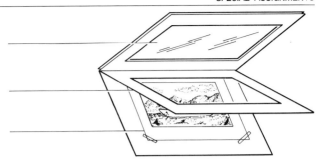

Acetate film sandwiched
between two 2 ply boards

4 ply window mount

Print mounted on 2 ply
backing

Above The illustration shows a specially designed storage matt. The print is mounted on a 2 ply board and covered with a 4 ply window mount. A protective layer made of a piece of acetate sandwiched between two 2 ply boards is hinged with tape on to the backing; this can be folded back if the print is to be framed.

Left This picture shows the visual impact which can be gained by using a matt overlay to enhance a photograph; compared with the unfinished print on the left, the final print has a more polished appearance.

Right There are various ways in which a print can be prepared for a portfolio. Unmounted pictures are best displayed in an album with acetate sleeves to protect the print's surface (centre). If prints are to be stored individually in a portfolio box they will require some form of protection: dry mounting on a card mount (top left) is the first stage in most methods; a matt overlay is an effective addition (top right); lamination, shown in the two bottom prints, offers almost complete protection at the cost of a slight loss in image quality, and is permanent, making it ideal if the prints will be handled constantly.

Photographs for decor

One of the nicest ways of using your best pictures is to display them on the walls of your home or office. Photographs lend themselves particularly well to this purpose since they can be made virtually any size, cropped to suit a particular space, and manipulated and selected to create a wide choice of colour effects. Even a single picture needs to be given careful consideration but often a group of pictures can be far more effective if they are chosen to complement each other.

Framing photographs can be both simple and inexpensive. Block mounting is perhaps the cheapest method; this involves mounting a photograph directly on a piece of blockboard, say ½ inch (1.3 cm) thick, and trimming it flush, after which the edges can be painted black. This is made even more simple by using the special self-adhesive polystyrene block mounts which are light enough to be supported on the wall with removable adhesive. A wide variety of self-assembly frame kits are also available, from simple clip frames where the print is sandwiched between glass

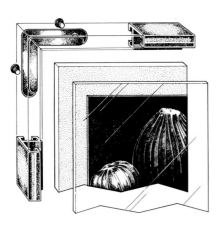

and hardboard held with small metal clips, to elaborate, professional-looking metal frames.

An effective and finished look can be given to a framed print by the use of a bevelled mat. An aperture is cut into a thick board and laid over the print; the colour of the mat can be chosen to complement both the photograph and the decor of the room. Even a large cork board with unmounted pictures pinned to it can provide an effective feature in an informal setting such as a work-room or kitchen, but with both a simple and a more elaborate display it is important to plan the position, sizes, and image quality of the individual pictures to create the optimum effect.

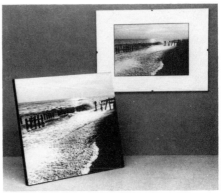

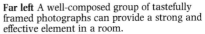

Far left A well-composed group of tastefully framed photographs can provide a strong and effective element in a room.

Above Two very simple and inexpensive methods of framing a photograph are block mounting on a self-adhesive board (bottom left), and sandwiching an unmounted print between a piece of glass and a hardboard backing fastened with metal clips (top right).

The illustrations show a block mount (top left), a clip frame (centre left), and a frame kit (bottom left).

Snowscapes

Weather conditions have a considerable influence on all pictures taken outdoors, both on the effect of the light and on the nature of the subject, but of all the climatic variations there is nothing that has such a dramatic impact as a fall of snow. To most photographers it is an irresistible subject, changing as it does the appearance of a familiar scene into something with an almost magical quality. However, to get the best pictures from a snow-covered countryside requires more than a little care and consideration since an all-white subject can easily become dull and uninteresting.

It is vital to have a focal point or centre of interest in a picture of a snowscape, even more than in other pictures, and since in most circumstances the image will be predominantly light in tone this usually means composing the picture around an object of a dark tone or bright colour. It is important to realize that unwanted dark tones or details in the photograph will become a distraction or a confusion. The abnormal presence of large areas of white in the image can also make

exposure calculation something of a problem since a reading taken in the normal way will give an extremely misleading measurement, resulting in considerable under-exposure. The safest method is to take a close-up reading from a detail of the scene which represents a mid-tone in the picture, or you can take an average from the snow itself and from a shadow area. Where the picture consists of all light tones with no shadow areas you can increase a reading taken in the normal way by 3 stops.

Another problem which can be encountered when shooting in colour is a blue cast caused by excess ultra-violet or blue sky reflected in the shadow areas; this can be overcome by the use of a warm filter such as a Wratten 81A or 81B. Although the most picturesque effects are obtained after a heavy fall of snow with the countryside looking like an iced cake and sunlight creating sparkling highlights, it can be even more effective when snow has only just started to fall and things are partially covered, leaving dark outlines and accentuating textures and shapes.

Opposite below A very graphic quality has been produced in this picture by calculating the exposure so that the snow forms a featureless white background, emphasizing the lines and shapes created by the building. Nikon F3; 105 mm lens; 1/125 at f5.6; Ilford XP1.

Left The essentially light tones of a snow scene mean that any dark tones become the focus of interest, as in this shot of two young musicians returning home. Rollei SLX; 150 mm lens; 1/125 at f5.6; Ilford FP4.

Left A woodland scene often creates quiet, delicate pictures after a fall of snow because the trees are isolated from their surroundings and the image is simplified. Rollei SLX; 150 mm lens; 1/60 at f8; Ilford FP4.

Recording a holiday

For most people a holiday is usually one of the more interesting and exciting events in the course of a year and an occasion when they invariably want to take photographs. All too frequently, however, these photographs fail to reflect the enjoyment and become instead a dreary succession of repetitive images. As with many other personal moments, a pleasing and evocative photographic record of a holiday will be of increasing value as time passes as well as a worthwhile project in itself. The main reason for the failure of many holiday records is that a lot of photographers, even experienced ones, unthinkingly fall into the trap of conventional, stereotyped pictures: the group of people smiling at the camera, the place of interest used only as a background to a shot, and a general lack of care in composition.

It is vital to apply the same amount of thought and photographic skill as you would to any other subject. Do not just take a picture from any spot, always make sure that you have the best viewpoint and that the picture is framed and composed effectively. Avoid posed and self-conscious portraits and look for candid, unobserved shots – people often pose automatically when they see a camera pointed at them, and if this happens let them think you have taken the picture but wait until they continue with what they were doing before actually taking it. Search for close-up images and long shots to give your pictures variety and pace, and also try to capture the mood and flavour of the place as well as its appearance. Take shots of local characters and activities such as fishermen on the beach or a festival or market.

Do not be tempted into taking a lot of equipment as this is likely to be a deterrent to carrying a camera with you all the time – and this is certainly the best way of recording a holiday, so that every spontaneous moment can be captured. Remember too that presentation is important and that a series of pictures carefully selected and laid out in an album will create a far better effect than an envelope full of unedited prints.

Above left A street festival has provided a record of a colourful moment during a holiday in Italy. A long-focus lens was used to isolate a small area of the scene and prevent the image from becoming too busy. Pentax S1A; 135 mm lens; 1/250 at f8; Ektachrome 64.

Left The relaxed atmosphere in the village square in St Paul de Vence as the evening game of boules gets under way forms the ideal setting for a picture evocative of the mood of this holiday. Pentax 6 × 7; 150 mm lens; 1/125 at f5.6; Ektachrome 200.

Above An isolated moment like the one captured in this shot of two children playing on the rocks can often be a more appealing record as well as a more satisfying picture. Nikon F3; 150 mm lens; 1/250 at f5.6; Ektachrome 64.

A photo-essay

Shooting a photo-essay is a valuable project as it can teach you how to explore a subject or a situation fully and can help you to discover different ways of creating images and revealing different aspects of a scene within the limitations of a given situation. Unlike a picture story which uses a linked series of pictures to describe a sequence of events, a photo-essay aims to 'build up' a picture of a subject or a situation by focusing the attention on individual aspects of it. While the photographs in a picture story must be essentially factual the individual images in a photo-essay can afford to be more ambiguous and evocative. Obviously you will choose a subject which you find both interesting and visually stimulating. It might be another hobby or a favourite place; even something as general as a season of the year or a day of the week could well provide a challenging and rewarding topic for your chosen project.

In order to give the essay variety and pace it is important to plan your pictures so that you can juxtapose close-up images with long shots, for instance; or look for shots with differing colour qualities and moods. Whether you intend to display the finished essay as a sequence of separate images or to mount them together as a layout you must consider the pictures in terms of how they interact with one another as well as how effective they are individually.

A photo-essay is an ideal starting-point for a picture wall (pp.174–5) or as part of a portfolio (pp.172–3), and as well as being a good way of extending your skills it will help you to develop a sense of design and, equally importantly, to apply a more critical and selective eye to your own work.

These pictures are part of a series taken in the village of Riquewihr in Alsace during the vintage. Collectively, the aim was to give a sense of the atmosphere of the occasion and the setting by isolating and juxtaposing certain aspects of the village and its activities with varied but complementary images. Nikon F3; varying lenses and exposures; Ilford XP1.

Above A photo-essay can be
shot in both black and white
and colour. Nikon F3; (top)
150 mm lens; 1/60 at f11;
(above) 150 mm lens; 1/30 at
f11; (right) 105 mm lens;
1/125 at f8; Ektachrome 64.

Manipulating the Image

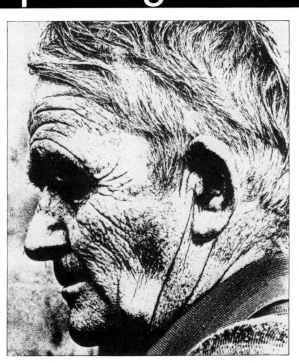

Tone separation

This technique produces an image in which the full range of tones of a normal negative are reproduced as three or four flat tones including black and white. It is also sometimes called 'posterization' since it tends to create very bold, simplified images with a strong graphic quality.

The first stage is to make two or three positives from your original negative on to Lith film; as they will have to be registered it is best to enlarge them to say 4 × 5 in. Registration is most easily achieved by the use of a punch and pin register board which you can make yourself (see diagram). Each of the sheets of Lith film should be punched and

located on the pin board prior to exposure. The object is to produce Lith positives, each representing a different range of tones in the original negative; a short exposure will produce an image in which only the darkest tones will record, a medium exposure will record the dark and middle tones, and a longer exposure will record all but the lightest tones. After processing, the positives should be checked for pinholes which should be spotted out using photopaque.

The next stage is to contact-print each of the positives in register on to a single sheet of normal continuous tone film such as Ilford FP4. First make a test strip from one of the

Above This series of pictures shows the stages in a tone separation in which an image of continuously variable tone is converted to one with just three tones – black, mid-grey, and white. From the left, the first picture shows the original photograph; next, the Lith negative produced by the short exposure which records the grey areas in the finished image; then, the Lith negative which was given the longer exposure and is responsible for recording the black tones; and last, the completed tone separation.

positives and select the exposure which produces a light grey. Using the register board with a sheet of continuous tone film taped into position, expose each of the positives in turn, giving the same exposure to each. When processed, the resulting negative will show the original dark tones as clear film, all the light tones as an even highlight tone, and all the tones between as a flat grey. With three Lith positives the mid-tones on the original will be shown as a light and a dark grey. It is also possible to produce a colour image by contacting the Lith positives on to a sheet of colour transparency film and using a different colour filter in the enlarger for each exposure.

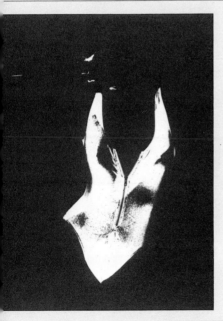

Left The diagram shows a simple and inexpensive register system using an office punch and a home-made register board.

Texture screens

There are occasions when a picture can be given additional impact by the use of a texture screen in combination with the negative or transparency from which the print is made. Texture screens can be obtained from many photographic dealers in sets containing a selection of 'surfaces' such as canvas or silk. The method is very straightforward: the screen and the negative are simply placed in contact with each other in the negative carrier of the enlarger and the print is made in the normal way.

In its most basic form the technique can be used simply to add a 'finish' to an image similar to that achieved by printing on to a textured enlarging paper. However, the process can have a more significant and interesting effect on the image, and making your own texture screen is one way of achieving this. Almost anything with a

Left A thin negative of a piece of cross-lit hessian was used in contact with the negative of this rural nude to add an element of texture.

Right These three pictures show the varied effect that can be produced by a texture screen when applied to the same negative. (Left) A piece of transparent tissue paper placed in contact with the printing paper. (Centre) A negative of a piece of sacking. (Right) A negative of a pile of coal.

Opposite below A small portion of a negative envelope was used to produce this effect.

relatively even-toned surface area can be used, a rough concrete wall, for instance, or an expanse of rippled sand on a beach.

If you use a light-toned surface such as an expanse of sand you will need to make a positive image from your negative on to a piece of film; the density and contrast of this image will have a considerable effect on the final image quality and you should experiment with different exposures and development times. If you choose a dark-toned surface such as leather or the bark of a tree it is possible to use the negative you make as the

texture screen; again it is advisable to bracket the exposures to provide a choice of effects.

In addition to using a texture screen in contact with the negative a larger sheet of translucent material such as tracing paper or textured glass can be used in contact with the printing paper. The advantage is that it can be removed before the exposure is complete, allowing a variety of effects. With colour print materials it is possible to create effects by using coloured surfaces and photographing them on transparency film or by toning or tinting black and white images.

Solarized prints

True solarization is the result of a massively over-exposed negative, and the effect which is now commonly called by this name is usually produced by a second exposure made during the development stage of the negative (or positive). The main features are the partial reversal of image and a white or black line dividing large areas of tone – this is in fact the Sabbatier effect, named after the man who discovered it. It can be done with a print although the effect often produces a considerable loss of contrast in the image; how-

ever, it is a good way of discovering the basic principles of the technique.

You make a print in the usual way using a harder grade of paper than would normally be required. Approximately half-way through the development the print must be re-exposed to 'white' light; usually one or two seconds from the ordinary room light is sufficient. The print can remain in the developer for this stage. Development is now completed and the print is fixed and washed in the normal way.

Right This effect was produced by re-exposing a negative made on Ilford FP4 from an original colour transparency about half-way through development; an exposure of 1 sec was given to the room light (100 watts) about 10 feet (3 metres) away. The resulting negative required an extra hard grade of paper.

More control can be achieved by re-exposing a negative or positive on film, but since the process is very unpredictable it is best not to use an original negative but to make a copy from a print or make a positive on film from the original negative; this can also be made on Lith film for a more extreme effect. The re-exposure must be made about half-way through the development time and the period of re-exposure found by trial and error (a film such as Ilford FP4 would require less exposure than a bromide paper because of its greater sensitivity).

Colour materials can be solarized in the same way, often with very startling results,

but of course you must process the film yourself. Colour prints, negatives, and transparencies can all be used but again the use of an original is not advisable. The effect can be varied further by the use of a coloured light source for re-exposure.

A similar effect to the Sabbatier can be created by the use of a special film called Agfa Contour on which the original negative or print can be copied and re-copied (Agfa issues a booklet on this film). Another way of producing pseudo-solarization is with a chemical solution produced by Tetenal called the Photografik Kit; this is used in conjunction with conventional processing procedures.

Left An original transparency was printed on Kodalith film which was re-exposed about half-way through development to produce this effect. The resulting solarized negative had good contrast and well-defined lines.

Left This pseudo-solarization was made by printing an Ektachrome transparency on Agfa Contour film. The effect of this film is controlled by the length of exposure which must be established by testing. Varying degrees of yellow filtration can be used to control the response of the film still further.

Montage prints

The ability to combine two or more images gives a photographer considerably more scope to express ideas and create effects than does a single straightforward picture, and this darkroom technique permits a far higher degree of control than, say, a double exposure or a slide sandwich. In simple terms, two or more negatives are printed on to the same sheet of paper, but skill is needed for the juxtaposition of the individual images and the shading and printing in, to allow the relevant details of the negatives to blend and separate where required.

Positioning the images is relatively simple. The first step is to tape a piece of drawing

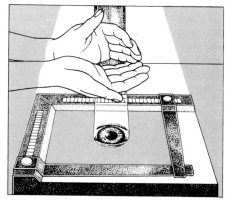

paper of the same size as the print you are going to make to the masking board of the enlarger and to size up and focus the first of your negatives. When this is satisfactory the main outlines of the images can be traced on to the paper with a felt-tip pen. At this stage you can make a test strip from the first negative. Next size up and focus the second negative and, using the traced outline of the first image, adjust the size and position of the second image so that it is aligned correctly. Make a test strip from the second negative. If only two images are being combined you can now attempt a first montage, but you must remember that the exposures will have a cumulative effect and where the images overlap the exposure of one or both its negatives must be reduced to avoid over-exposure. It is

also very important to mark one corner of the printing paper so that it can be placed back on the easel exactly the same way round for each exposure.

The essence of an effective montage lies in the balance between the individual images, and this can be controlled by shading; where you want one image to dominate you must 'hold back' or shade out the relevant area of the other negative either using a piece of card cut to shape or with your hand; where you want two images to blend you must 'vignette' the edge of the image by moving a piece of card gently during the exposure so that each edge graduates off to white where the other begins. You may need several attempts with this type of image before you produce a satisfactory result.

Far left These four pictures are the images from which the final montage print was made. Each picture was sized and a tracing of the main outlines made on a piece of paper the size of the finished print.

Left This is the final montage effect involving four separate exposures on to one piece of paper; unwanted areas of each of the individual negatives were shaded out during the exposures.

Opposite above The illustration shows how one area of a negative can be shaded out with the hands.

Photograms

In its simplest form a photogram is the silhouetted shape of an object created by placing it on a piece of photographic paper and exposing it to light either from an enlarger without a negative or from a light bulb suspended above it. With a solid or opaque object all you will get is a white shape on a black background, but even this can produce an effective image if the object has an interesting outline or if a number of objects are arranged into a pleasing composition. The objects do not have to be flat as even a round or solid object will cast a sharp shadow from a small light source, as through an enlarger lens.

If you make your photograms on to a paper with a fairly thin base such as a single-weight bromide it is a simple matter after processing and drying to use this as a negative and to make a contact print on to another piece of paper, thereby producing a black image of the object on a white background. Photograms are incidentally a good way of using any outdated or partially fogged paper you may have.

In addition to purely black and white images it is also possible to create pictures with a range of tones by selecting objects which have varying degrees of translucency – tinted or clear glass objects, for example – or which have a textural quality such as paper or thin fabric. As well as producing photograms by contact it is also possible to use small objects or pieces of things and make enlarged photograms by placing them in the negative carrier of the enlarger and projecting the image on to the paper. In this way images of quite considerable impact and beauty can be produced from quite mundane objects such as a feather or a pressed flower. Colour materials can also be used, either coloured objects or colour filters. Reversal materials such as Cibachrome will produce images against a white background and negative positive paper against black.

Apart from their appeal as images in their own right photograms can also be used as a basis for texture screens (pp. 186–7) and as elements in a slide sandwich (pp. 204–5), back projection (pp. 30–1) and glass montage (pp. 28–9). Black and white photograms can be toned and tinted to add further interest (pp. 200–1 and 216–17).

Right The illustrations show four different methods of making a photogram: (top left) the enlarger is used as a light source; (top right) the light source is a lamp used at an oblique angle; (below left) a flashlight with a paper cone fastened on one end is used to create a very directional light; (below right) a light bulb is suspended above the photographic paper.

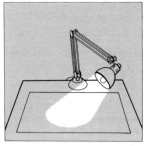

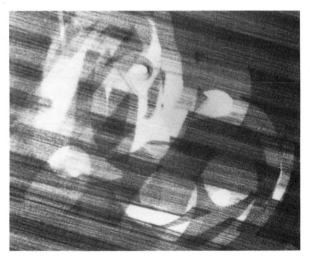

Above left A completely abstract image was formed by placing a variety of card and acetate strips on a piece of reeded glass supported just above a sheet of bromide paper and exposed by an obliquely angled light source.

Far left This image was created by sprinkling a few sugar crystals on the glass negative carrier of the enlarger and projecting them directly on to the bromide paper with the enlarger at maximum magnification.

Left A flashlight fitted with a cardboard snoot was used to 'paint' this photogram of an antique bottle which was laid on to the bromide paper.

Above This simple image has been created by the most basic method – contact-printing. In this case a lace doily was printed directly on a sheet of bromide paper. The success of this method depends on the interest of the object in terms of shape, translucency, and texture.

Line-sketch prints

This process converts a normal negative into an image which closely resembles that produced by pen and ink or scraper boards, that is a fine white or black line on a contrasting background. You need a very sharp negative of a subject which contains clearly defined details and boldly separated tones. If your negative is of a fairly small format – 35 mm, or even $2\frac{1}{4}$ inch square – it is worth making an enlarged positive on to a normal sheet film of say 4×5 in; Ilford FP4 is ideal. From this you must make a contact negative ensuring that glass and film surfaces are dust free; this should be of normal density and contrast.

After processing, the two films must be registered precisely and taped into position, with the two films back to back and the emulsions on the outside. This is crucial since it is the separation between the images which creates the effect: the sandwich should resemble an even-toned dark grey piece of film.

This should then be contact-printed on to a piece of Lith film and processed in Lith developer according to the manufacturer's instructions. However, unlike a conventional contact print this must be made with an obliquely angled light, say 3 feet or so (a metre) to one side and at an angle of 45° to the horizontal. The light source should be sharp and hard – a projector or spotlight is ideal – and the contact frame must be rotated on a turntable during the exposure, which must be established by trial and error.

The resulting image will be a fine black line on clear film and if required this can be contact-printed on to another piece of Lith film which will produce a black line on a white background on the print. Colour can be introduced by toning or dyeing the resulting print or by printing on to a colour base paper (pp. 216–17). A non-photographic way of achieving a similar result is to trace and shade the main details of the subject on a light print using a waterproof ink and then bleaching away the photographic image using a potassium ferricyanide bleach solution.

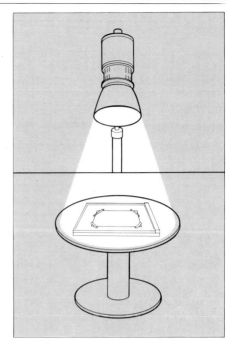

Opposite below To produce this image of a tree, an enlarged positive was first made on to 8 × 10 Lith film from a 35 mm negative; from this a Lith negative was made by contact and the resulting combination contact-printed on to a hard grade of paper.

Opposite above The original 35 mm negative was enlarged to 4 × 5 on FP4 film and the resulting positive contact-printed to give a negative of the same size; the two were then sandwiched together back to back in register and contact-printed on to Lith film using the obliquely angled light source described, and the print made from the result.

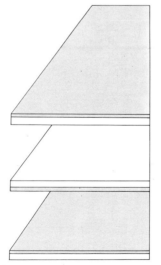

Above The illustration shows the set-up used to make a line-sketch print. The spotlight, which is at a 45° angle, is directed on to the film which is taped on a contact frame positioned on a turntable.

Left This is a magnified section of the film sandwich made to produce a line-sketch print (see picture opposite above).

Distorted prints

There are a number of ways in which a normal negative or print can be distorted to produce effects ranging from the slightly odd to the abstract. The simplest way of doing this is to alter the angle of the bromide paper on the base-board of the enlarger; instead of it being parallel to the negative carrier as intended you can use supports to tilt the masking board holding the paper at a steep angle. The effect will vary according to the direction of the slope in relation to the image

on the negative. You will have to use a small aperture on the lens in order to obtain a reasonably sharp image over the length of the print, and if your enlarger has a tilting negative carrier this can be used to offset the changing plane of focus on the print. (This technique can also be used to *correct* negatives with converging verticals.)

By dispensing with the masking board and taping or clipping the paper directly to supports such as blocks of wood it is possible to

Above The 'long legs' effect in this shot was produced by tilting the masking board so that the printing paper was held at an acute angle.

Right The diagram shows two methods of creating distortion by altering the angle of the paper: (top) to give the 'long legs' effect, and (bottom) by curving the paper.

twist and curl the paper to obtain distortion in more than one direction. Other ways of producing distortion at the printing stage include altering the magnification of the enlarger during exposure, rotating or moving the paper along during the exposure, and printing through hammered or patterned glass.

It is also possible to distort prints by cutting and reassembling them. One amusing approach is to make two identical prints of a full-face portrait with one of them reversed, and to cut each print precisely down the centre and butt the opposite halves of the print (the same sides of the face); this underlines quite dramatically the lack of symmetry in the human face. Other variations involve cutting a print into parallel strips and slightly displacing them before re-forming the print and mounting it on to board. The displacement can be made either by separating the strips slightly or by joining the edges and offsetting them laterally. It is also possible to intersperse two different prints cut into identical strips or to mix strips cut from prints of the same subject which have been toned different colours. Instead of strips you can also cut the print into irregular shapes or circles.

Top The zoom effect of this image is created by racking back the enlarging lens while the print is being exposed. This both enlarges the image and throws it out of focus.

Above This effect is produced by making two prints from a negative, one of them reversed left to right. Each print is then cut down the centre, and the two halves rejoined.

Print patterns

It is possible to make very intriguing, abstract images from quite straightforward pictures to produce striking and decorative results. The technique is quite simple and you will in many cases find suitable material from your existing photographs although it is fun to plan your images in advance and to shoot pictures specially for the purpose. You will need a sharp craft knife, a steel straight edge, a cutting surface, some photo adhesive, and a mounting board. The best pictures to use are those which consist of bold shapes and lines with a clearly defined subject and an uncluttered background. The technique will suit a wide variety of subjects from landscapes to nudes.

The basic approach is to make two prints from your selected negative; they should be identical in size, density, and contrast, but one of them should be reversed left to right (this is achieved by turning the negative the other way up in the enlarger). After processing and drying, the prints should be trimmed

carefully and identically using the knife and the straight edge. You will now find that they can be butted together along any one of their four sides according to the subject and mounted on to a board to create a symmetrical image. In some instances with a fairly symmetrical subject you may find it more effective not to reverse one of the prints. More elaborate patterns can be created by using four, six, or even more prints. Four prints, with two of them reversed, can be joined together in a square, for example, or they can be joined together alternately in a line to create a frieze effect.

This technique can be used equally effectively with both colour and black and white pictures; black and white pictures can be toned in different colours to add a further dimension to the pattern. Images like this can be formed to good effect for display purposes and could also be copied and reprinted on to a photo-linen material (pp. 210–11) for use as cushion covers for instance.

Left With this type of image, the photograph has to be taken specially so that the horizon or dominant lines in the image run diagonally. Here, four prints were made with two reversed and joined as shown.

Below This image was produced by making four prints with two of them reversed left to right; they were then butted together alternately.

Hand-coloured prints

The technique of hand-colouring black and white prints was first evolved through necessity, there being no colour film in the early days of photography, and the purpose then was to find a substitute for, or an imitation of, the real thing. Today of course there is little point in trying to recreate the original colours of a scene by hand-colouring but it does offer considerable scope for unusual or intriguing results.

The best colouring mediums, and the easiest to use, are the clear photo-colour dyes which can be applied with a brush and mixed and diluted to control the hue and depth of colour. Take some care in selecting your print for colouring: avoid images with high contrast and pictures which have large areas of dark tone since it will be impossible to

colour over them. It is preferable to make a print with lighter than normal tones. Many people like to apply a sepia tone to the print before colouring, but this is not vital. A matt or semi-matt surface is best as this will 'take' the colour better. It is also advisable to make an identical spare print so that you can first test the colours before applying them to the finished print. Unless you are particularly skilful with a brush it is a good idea to avoid images that contain a lot of fine detail and intricate outlines and also pictures with large areas of even tone as these will show up any unevenness in application of the colour.

You will need a selection of good-quality sable brushes ranging in size from large, say No. 10, to a small No. 1 or 0. Cotton balls are useful as are cotton buds and a sheet or two

of photographic blotting paper; you will also need a palette for mixing colours and of course a container of water. Your working area should be well lit by daylight. Mount the print on a board or fix it by means of adhesive tape before you start work.

Before you attempt to add colour dampen the surface of the print with a cotton ball soaked in clear water and blot any surplus away – this will help the dyes to 'take' evenly. Mix your colours to the required effect on the palette, trying them first on the spare print, and aim to achieve the correct depth and tone in one application. Start with the larger areas of colour, working down to the small details requiring the fine brush. Large areas can be coloured by swabbing with a cotton ball or bud. Intricate details can be coloured by using a waterproof masking solution which will protect unwanted areas from the dye and can be peeled away later.

Right A sepia-toned black and white print on resin-coated paper was used as the basis for this photograph, with only a single area of colour being added to the bloom. This sort of effect requires only a minimum of skill with a brush.

Above right The materials necessary for hand-colouring arc photo-colour dyes, a range of brushes, cotton balls and buds, blotting paper, a palette, water, and a mounting board.

Left The aim in this picture of a girl was for an almost natural effect, but the colours are just sufficiently unreal to give the image a slightly intriguing quality.

Collage

Collage is a way of combining a number of individual images in one picture by cutting and mounting elements of separate photographs together. The basic method is to use one picture as a background with areas from other photographs mounted on it. This technique can be used to create totally unreal abstract images or pictures which appear to be realistic and unmanipulated. The latter requires careful control over the individual elements; the perspective and lighting of each individual shot must be totally compatible and the actual artwork carried out with great care. In most circumstances such pictures must be planned in advance and taken specifically for the purpose, and then printed to size to a working layout.

Where realism is not the aim, there is far greater flexibility in the choice of images and the way they are juxtaposed, and often existing prints can be used. Not all of the elements need be of photographic origin – sections of photographs could be mounted on a patter-ned fabric background, or images cut from magazines or drawings could be incorporated into a photographic background. The only limitation is your own imagination.

The main requirements are scissors, a craft knife with spare blades, a cutting surface, an adhesive such as a spray photo mountant, mounting board for the background picture, and fine sandpaper. You also need brushes and retouching medium for making good the edges. The background picture should first be mounted, and the images to be cut will be most easily handled if printed on a single-weight paper. It is also a good idea to make a few spare prints at the same time to allow for errors. After the images have been cut out, chamfer the edges by rubbing the back of the images gently with fine sandpaper; then coat them with adhesive and stick them down. On completion and after retouching, the composite can be rephotographed and printed to a smaller size to minimize any visible handiwork.

Left The illustration shows the main items used to produce the collage: the individual prints roughly cut out, marker pen, small sharp scissors and craft knife for making the final cut, fine sandpaper for chamfering the edges, the working tracing of the images, and spray mountant.

Right This composite picture consists of six individual prints which were cut out and pasted together into position. A preliminary sketch was made based on the original negatives and then prints made to correct size on single-weight paper to minimize the edge effect. The complete montage was retouched to hide the joins and rephotographed. In this picture the copy negative was reticulated, immersed in hot water, to give the textured effect and to add to the surrealistic mood of the image.

Making a slide sandwich

This is a way of combining two or more images, but unlike a double exposure the effect can be assessed visually and the images can be selected and juxtaposed in the comfort of your home. The basic requirement is two or more transparencies of less than normal density and a light box or illuminated surface upon which the transparencies can be manoeuvred. In the first instance it is possible to make a sandwich from reject transparencies but in the long run it is far better to plan your images in advance and shoot trans-

parencies that fulfil any special requirements you may have.

Essentially, a slide sandwich builds up tones and details by the addition of the second and subsequent images. The most basic type of sandwich, and the easiest to control, is one where you have a clearly defined subject against a light and uncluttered background and a second transparency which consists of a fairly subtle textured or patterned tone. Unlike a double exposure a slide sandwich works on the principle that a

darker tone or detail on one image will 'read through' a light tone on the other.

It is a good idea to sort the transparencies into categories before you start a session: one category should contain pictures with a boldly defined main subject against a light or clear background, another fairly light, even-toned images of subtle colour, and another images with textures or patterns. It helps to have slides of different formats, both 35 mm and $2\frac{1}{4}$ in square; this will give you scope to manoeuvre and juxtapose the images.

Once you have positioned the transparencies to your liking tape them together carefully at the edges. The simplest method of presentation is to mount them together in a slide mount and project them; alternatively, the sandwich can be used to produce a colour print, but the most satisfactory method is to make a duplicate transparency from the sandwich. This can be done relatively inexpensively by a colour laboratory or you can make your own duplicates (pp.208–9) by using a slide duplicator or with the aid of an enlarger using sheets of duplicating film which can be obtained from Kodak. However, as preliminary tests will be necessary this is not practicable unless you have to make a number of duplicates at once or do this type of work frequently.

Left This image was produced by combining a transparency of a lake scene with one of a rain-spattered window.

Above A nude torso photographed against a white background in the studio has been juxtaposed with a seascape to create this rather surrealistic picture.

High-contrast effects

One of the most basic ways in which you can manipulate the image quality and the mood of a picture is to alter the contrast. In normal circumstances a black and white print is made on a grade of paper which matches the tonal range of the negative, the end result being an image where there is a full range of tones with detail in all but the densest shadows and brightest highlights. By deliberately selecting a harder grade of paper than the negative requires it is possible to produce an image of a quite different quality and to give emphasis to particular aspects of the image. A normal negative will yield a full range of tones on the normal grade of paper (Grade 2), but it is possible to buy enlarging papers up to Grade 5.

The effect of an increase in contrast is to make the light tones of the image lighter and the dark tones darker, and this alone can often add a considerable degree of impact. In addition, by varying the exposure it is possible to give emphasis to either the lighter or darker range of tones at the expense of the other; for instance, with a portrait printed on a Grade 5 paper and given additional exposure for the highlights the effect would be to reproduce the lighter skin tones as harsh, boldly defined areas with the shadow areas recorded as black or near-black tones. The increase of contrast will also have a quite dramatic effect on the textural quality of the picture and also on the grain of the film, making it much more prominent.

If you find that using a harder grade of paper does not give sufficient contrast then it is possible to copy a normal print and to under-expose and over-develop the copy negative to achieve the desired effect. In some instances it can be effective to reproduce an image in just pure black and white tones, and this can be done quite simply by using special Lith film or paper in conjunction with special Lith developer. By printing directly on to this material and processing according to the instructions all the tones in the original negative, or positive, will be transposed into black and white without further manipula-

tion. The exposure is important since it determines at which point in the range of tones on the original the division between black and white occurs on the Lith version. A short exposure, for instance, will leave all but the darkest tones as white, whereas a longer exposure will record all but the lightest tones as black. This technique is most suitable for subjects with a bold and interesting outline or with a strong element of pattern or texture.

Left This picture of the cathedral in Barcelona was produced by making a Lith positive from the original black and white negative, making a Lith negative from this, and then making the final print.

Above These two prints made on Agfa Brovira Grade 5 show how the effect of exposure influences the image quality: the shorter exposure emphasizes the mid-tones and shadows but loses detail in the highlights; the longer exposure accentuates the highlights and mid-tones at the cost of the shadow detail.

Right These two pictures demonstrate how a photograph can be given additional impact by printing on to a hard grade of paper, in this case the comparison is between Grade 2 and Grade 5.

Making duplicate transparencies

There are often occasions when you need to have a duplicate transparency of one of your pictures, to produce a copy for a friend for instance. Most laboratories offer a slide duplicating service at quite reasonable cost, but it is not at all difficult to produce your own, and the advantages are considerable. You can, for example, alter the colour balance of your original either to correct a fault or to create a more dramatic effect. You can also 'crop' your transparencies in the same way as a print from a negative to exclude unwanted details, create emphasis, or improve composition. In addition you can use duplicate transparencies to produce double exposure effects with more control than you can achieve when shooting a 'live' subject.

The key to successful and simple slide duplicating is the special film produced for the purpose by Kodak called Type 5071; this is available in 35 mm bulk lengths and also in sheet film. It is balanced for use with tungsten light, and although it does not have an ISO rating ISO 16/13° is a suitable starting point for test exposures. An SLR camera is really essential although the sheet film can be used very successfully in an enlarger with the transparency placed in the negative carrier

and projected in the same way as if you were making a colour print. Alternatively, you could contact-print the transparencies on to the sheet film, although obviously this will not allow any cropping or enlarging.

It is possible to buy slide copying attachments to fit most SLR cameras at a modest cost. The light source can be provided by a photoflood bulb or a quartz halogen lamp. An alternative method is to make a simple light box with a perspex screen and use the camera fitted with a macro lens, bellows, or extension tubes to obtain the necessary degree of magnification, although this system will require very careful alignment.

Exposure calculation is most easily carried out using TTL metering as this will take into account changes in magnification but in the first instance a series of test exposures will be needed to establish exposures and filtration. For this you will need a set of colour printing filters which should be used between the light source and the diffusing screen. The filtration will vary according to the film type being copied but once established it should remain the same for normal transparencies on the same stock; however, different film types may require different filtration.

Right The illustration shows two slide copying devices: (top) a simple, relatively inexpensive attachment using a supplementary lens and a sliding tube which offers a limited degree of magnification control and fits on to the camera lens; (bottom) a more flexible unit designed as an accessory for a bellows close-up attachment. Both units need an even source of light of the correct colour temperature to provide suitable illumination.

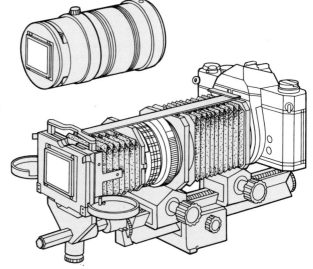

Above These two pictures show how a photograph can often be improved by cropping, something which is done frequently in black and white photography. With colour transparencies, cropping can be carried out when making an enlarged duplicate.

Left A change in the colour balance of a photograph can add impact to a picture. This is also easy with a slide duplicator. Once the correct filtration has been established changes can be made by simply adding the required colour correction filter to the pack.

Printing on different surfaces

In addition to printing an image on conventional printing papers a variety of other materials can be used quite successfully. One of the simplest methods is to print on to photo-linen, a white woven fabric which is coated with a photographic emulsion and can be used in the same way as bromide paper; once processed it can be put to various functional and decorative uses such as cushion covers, curtains, and decorative patches

for clothing. A number of manufacturers supply this material. Although the resulting image is of course in black and white, colour can be introduced by means of fabric dyes and chemical toners (pp. 216–17); as well as printing conventional subjects it can be interesting to experiment with photographic patterns and texture pictures to create a more abstract or subtle effect.

Another ready-made printing material

which can be obtained from a number of photographic suppliers is Metone, a photosensitized aluminium sheet; it is available in different sizes and thicknesses and in both matt and burnished surfaces. Like photo-linen, the material can be treated and processed in a similar way to bromide paper but you should not use an acid stop bath or fixer as these could react with the metal. It is also possible to dye and tone images on this material.

The greatest flexibility is possible with the use of liquid silver halide emulsion which can be used to make almost any surface light-sensitive. A number of manufacturers supply this material and full instructions are included. The emulsion is solid at room temperature and must be immersed in warm water to liquify it; it must be coated and dried in safelight conditions. Some surfaces will have to be primed before the emulsion is applied – make sure they are clean. A subbing solution is usually supplied with the emulsion which is suitable for non-porous surfaces such as ceramics; most other surfaces can be primed with polyurethane varnish.

Far left The decoration on this plate was produced by coating the inside surface with a liquid emulsion and, once it had dried, exposing a negative in the usual way on the sensitized plate and processing it. In this case the circular image was produced by using a negative shot on a fish-eye lens.

Left This picture shows how a negative printed on an emulsion which was specially coated on a linen base can be used for practical purposes, in this case as a cushion cover. After processing, the photo/fabric can – with care – be sewn, washed, and ironed in the normal way.

211

Gum bichromate prints

This is one of the early photographic processes and is possible only with contact printing as it requires long exposures either to sunlight or an ultra-violet lamp. An enlarged negative can, however, be made from an original either on to film or bromide paper although the latter will require even longer printing times. You will need good-quality drawing paper with a suitable texture which must be cut to size, soaked thoroughly, and then taped to a piece of board so that it shrinks and dries absolutely flat. The paper must then be sized with gelatin; dissolve 1 oz (28 g) of gelatin powder in 250 cc of water, allow it to set and then remelt it and brush it

evenly on to the paper. Next it must be sensitized; the solutions required are a saturated solution of powdered gum arabic and a saturated solution of potassium bichromate made and stored in separate containers. The only other material required is a selection of powder colours such as Winsor and Newton – a tin each of red, blue, and yellow will allow you to mix almost any colour.

The next stage is to mix equal parts of the gum arabic and potassium bichromate solutions, adding the required powder colour and mixing thoroughly; this must from now on be stored in light-proof containers. Apply the sensitizer to the paper in subdued light; it can

Right This nude was printed using a single coating of emulsion on a textured water-colour paper with Winsor and Newton burnt umber water-colour powder. The 8 × 10 negative made on Ilford FP4 sheet film from an original Ektachrome transparency required an exposure of 40 minutes under an ultra-violet lamp.

Far right Two coatings and two exposures were made to produce this woodland scene, the first with a purple pigment and the second with brown. The negative had to be carefully registered for the second exposure.

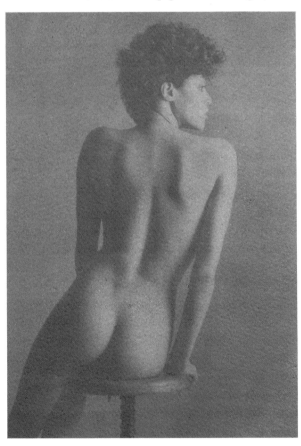

either be brushed on using a conventional household paint-brush or pad, or for a smoother finish use an artist's camel-hair or sable brush, but note that the brush strokes can contribute to the effect of the image when the paper is dry. The paper should be dried in darkness.

The exposure must be made by sandwiching the enlarged negative in contact with the sensitized paper in a contact frame or clamping it between glass and fibreboard. It will require two to three hours' exposure in sunlight or about half an hour if you are using an ultra-violet lamp. The print is processed by rinsing it gently in a dish of cold water for an hour or so until the unexposed pigment is washed away. This can be speeded up by spraying the print with water or gently brushing it with a soft-haired brush but this should be done extremely carefully as otherwise the gelatin and pigment may be dislodged from the paper.

Hand-made negatives

Photograms are one way of making images without the aid of a camera, but another is to make negatives from which a number of prints can be taken in the normal way, rather than to create the images directly on to the paper. This method has the added advantage that, unlike photograms, the composition can be made in normal room light. The basic technique involves the use of a variety of coloured and clear fluids to form patterns and shapes directly on to a piece of glass or translucent material; $2\frac{1}{4}$ inch or 35 mm glass slide

mounts are ideal, as they can be washed clean and used again.

The choice of fluids is largely a question of the pigment tone and pattern required; water-colour inks are an ideal medium to start with and they can be dropped on to the glass from an eye dropper. Since the aim is to obtain interesting swirls and textures it is a good idea to mix both other colours and other fluids with your main pigment to achieve this effect: a small drop of detergent, for example, will cause the water-colour to form shapes

Right A mixture of water-colour ink, detergent, and transparent glue were sandwiched together between two pieces of cling film and manipulated while still liquid to create this almost under-water effect.

Opposite left Two different colours of water-colour ink were combined with household bleach on a glass slide and the result blotted gently with a piece of paper to produce a slightly textured effect in this abstract.

Opposite right This image was produced by allowing small drops of water-colour ink, transparent glue, and detergent to intermingle on a glass slide, and making a print from the resulting transparency.

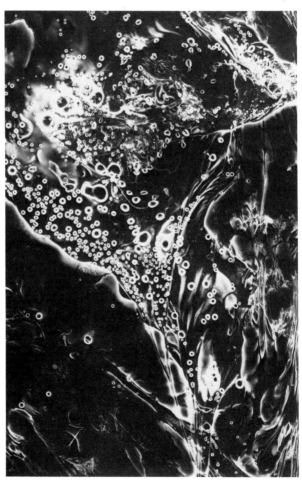

and shading, and household bleach can also produce interesting effects. As you will be making prints from these 'negatives' you must judge the effect in terms of density and contrast as for an ordinary negative.

One way of producing interesting patterns and textures is to press two pieces of glass together with the pigment inside and then carefully draw them apart; if you add a drop of detergent or transparent glue to make the pigment more glutinous this can create a wide range of effects. Further variations can be introduced by using a base material other than glass; a thin translucent paper, for instance, can add texture to the final effect as

well as causing the pigments to react in a different way, and it can be effective to use thin acetate or freezer wrap which can be crinkled when the pigment has been applied and then pulled apart when it has started to dry.

Although the negatives can look very effective in black and white, with different-coloured pigments it is possible to print them on to colour materials, either on to transparency film or negative or positive paper, depending upon the effect you want. Images which are made in this way can be incorporated into a montage or a double exposure, perhaps in combination with conventional photographic images.

Left The materials needed to make your own negatives include water-colour inks and a range of brushes. An eye dropper is ideal for dropping the ink on to the glass.

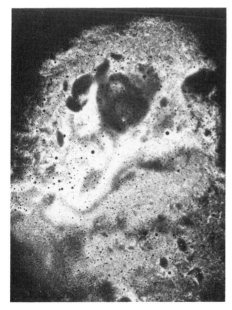

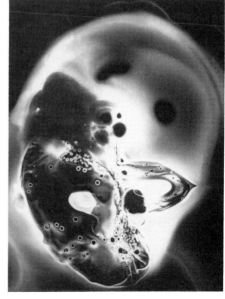

Toning black and white prints

There are a variety of methods for producing a coloured image from a black and white negative. The most familiar is probably the application of a sepia tone where a conventionally made black and white print is bleached, washed, and then re-developed in special solutions. This can produce an image with a very pleasing quality and lends itself well to pictures with a romantic or period flavour. Some toners such as selemium or gold have only a slight effect on the colour of the image but greatly improve the permanence of the print.

There is also a wide variety of chemical toners available which can be used to produce a range of colours from yellow through to orange, green, and blue. The effect with chemical toning is to convert the darker tones to a colour, leaving the whites unaffected, but it is also possible to produce images on a tinted paper in which the whites and lighter tones have the predominant colour cast and the darker tones are less affected. A number of manufacturers produce these papers in a choice of tints including metallic gold and fluorescent.

A similar effect can be achieved by immersing a conventional black and white print in a fabric dye bath; if the dye is made fairly dilute the build-up of colour can be judged quite easily and the print removed when the desired effect has been achieved. A particularly versatile kit of chemicals containing a mixture of bleaches, toners, and dyes is available under the name of ColorVir in Britain. These solutions can be used singly or in conjunction to give a wide range of effects including a multi-coloured effect and something similar to solarization.

In addition to dyeing and toning black and white prints it is also possible to use most of the same solutions on black and white negatives or positives on film, thereby producing transparencies; by sandwiching together two or more of these of the same image in register, but treated differently, even wider possibilities are available. These techniques are particularly suitable with prints for display and decorative purposes as they can be used to create bold graphic images; another possible use is in the production of greetings cards and calendars.

Left A conventional two-bath sepia toner (bleach and re-developer) was used to produce the effect on this nude shot, emphasizing its rather whimsical quality.

Above Use of the ColorVir solarization solution was followed by red dye treatment and then partial sulphurization to produce this image. The negative was also printed through a texture screen.

Right The two-colour effect of this image resulted from using the solarizing solution, followed by blue toning from the ColorVir kit.

Bibliography

Photofinish, *Alex Morrison*. Michael Joseph.
Composition in Colour Photography, *Wim Noordhoek*. Argus Books.
Nude and Glamour Photography, *Michael Busselle*. Macdonald; Simon & Schuster.
Photographing People, *Michael Busselle*. Mitchell Beazley; Simon & Schuster.
Wild Life in Britain. Automobile Association.
Sunday Times Book of the Countryside, Macdonald.
Photographer's Handbook, *John Hedgecoe*. Ebury Press.
Darkroom Handbook, *Michael Langford*. Ebury Press.
Special Effects Photography, *Michael Langford*. Ebury Press.
Alternative Photographic Processes, *Kent Wade*. Morgan & Morgan.
Creative Camera Techniques, *Axel Bruck*. Focal Press.
Darkroom Dynamics, *Jim Stone*. Newnes Technical Books.
Agfacontour Professional. Agfa-Gevaert.
Travellers' France. *Arthur Eperon*. Pan Books.
Travellers' Italy. *Arthur Eperon*. Pan Books.
The Book of the Seaside. Automobile Association.
Photography Pocket Guide, *Michael Busselle*. Octopus Books.
Photography – A Handbook of History, Materials and Processes, *Charles Swedlund*. Holt, Rinehart & Winston.
Beyond Photography, *Jack Tait*. Focal Press.
Effects and Experiments in Photography, *Paul Petzold*. Focal Press.
Creative Camera Techniques, *Axel Bruck*. Focal Press.
Walking Old Railways, *Christopher Somerville*. David & Charles.
Dialogue with Photography, *Paul Hill and Thomas Cooper*. Thames & Hudson.
On Photography, *Susan Sontag*. Penguin Books.
Photodiscovery, *Bruce Bernard*. Thames & Hudson.
The Magic Image, *Cecil Beaton and Gail Buckland*. Little, Brown & Co.
World Photography, *Bryn Campbell*. Hamlyn.

Index

Numbers in italics refer to captions

A

Abstract image 10
  nude *17*, 148–9, *149*
Advertising photography 164, 165
Agfa Contour film 189
Album, photograph 172, *173*
Animal photography 52, *53*, 70, *70, 71*, 76, *76*, 77, 82–3, *82*, 90, 93, 124, 126
Architectural photography 54–5, *54*, 55, 60–1, *60*, *61*, 89, 138, *139*
Atmospheric haze 39, 102, 114

B

Back projection 29–30, *31*, 193
Bellows unit 19, 142, 208
Bird's-eye view photography 113–14, *115*
Black and white photography
  filters for 46–7, *47*
  prints *see* Prints
Black-light lamp 20
Block mounting 174, *175*
Blur 14, *15*, 40, *41*, 42, *42*, 93
Bold colour effect 130–1, *131*
Box camera 169
Bracketing exposures 23, 38, 40, 44, 45, 154, *155*, 187
Buildings, photographing *see* Architectural photography

C

Calendar photography 166–7, *167*, 217
Camera, box 169
  pinhole 168–9, *168, 169*
  shake 81, 122, 141, 142
    controlled 41
  SLR 9, 37, 133, 136, 142, 168, 208
  techniques 7–50
  viewfinder 9, 122, 124, 142

Canvas screen 186
Car, photographing from 76
Child photography 80–1, *80*, *81*, 124
Children's playground, photographing 80–1, *80*, *81*
Circus photography 96–7, *96*, *97, 98*
City photography *see* Town photography
Close-up photography 19, 62, 70, 97, 110, *110, 111*, 140, 142, *143, 144*
Collage 202, *202*
Colour
  balance 12, 14, 208, *209*
  contrast 118, 126, 128, 130, 138
  effect, bold 130–1, *131*
  false 26–7, *26, 27*
  and mood 118, *119*
  photography, tri- 32, *33*
  saturation 118, 131
Composition 108, 112, 126, 136, 138, 141
Contact print 156–7, *157*, 158, 160, 184, 192, *193*, 195, 208, 212
Contact sheet mosaic 156–7, *157*
Contrast 54, 206, *207*
  colour *see* Colour contrast
Cropping 110, *111*, 208, *209*
Crystals, polarized 18, 19, *19*

D

Decor, photography for 174–5, *175*
Depth of field 8, 66, 82, 110, 141, 142
Developing *see* Film processing
Diffraction grating 171, *171*
Diffusing screen 148
Displaying prints 172, *173*, 174–5, *175*
Distorted image 10, *67*
  prints 196–7, *196, 197*
Double exposure 28, 36–7, *36*, *37*, 166–7, 171, 204, 215
Duplicating slides 205, 208, *208, 209*

Dye, fabric 210, 217
  photo-colour 200, *201*

E

Exposure
  bracketing 23, 38, 40, 44, 45, 154, *155*, 187
  calculation 36, 55, 55, 97, 102, 104, 113, 120, 122, 123, 124, 129, 146, 154, 156, 160, 169, 171, 176, 177, 206, *207*, 208, 212
  double 28, 36–7, *36*, *37*, 166–7, 171, 204, 215
  effects 44–5, *45*
  meter 44, 97, 132–3
  multiple image 21, 36–7, *37*, 64
  time 24, *24*, 25, 48–9, *49*, 170
Extension tube 62, *62*, 142, *142*, 208

F

Fabric dye 210, 217
False colour effect 26–7, *26*, *27*
Farm photography 90, *91*
Film
  Agfa Contour 189
  black and white 46, 120, 123, 129, 146, 184
  choice of 55, 107
  colour balance 12
  colour transparency 27, 55, 120, 123, 129, 170, 185
  daylight 23
  duplicating 205, 208
  fast 23, 34, *35*, 35, 54, 55, 81, 97, 107
  infra-red 38–9, *38, 39*
  instant picture 150, *151*
  Lith 184, 185, 189, 195, 206
  processing 26, 27, 34, 35, 97, 107
  slow 123, 138
  tungsten light 16, 23, *26*
Filter
  colour 12, *12*, *13*, 14, *15*, 22, 26, 27, *27*, 32, 37,

39, *39*, 46–7, *47*, 114,
146, 155, 157, 170, 176,
185
colour correction 27
colour printing 208
colour separation 32
daylight-to-tungsten
conversion 16
factor 46
fog 107
graduated 146, *147*, 155
neutral density 40–1, 146
pastel 107
polarizing 18, 64, 66, 114,
131, *131*, 146, *147*
star-burst 171
ultra-violet 22, 114
use for black and white film
46, *47*, *47*
Fish-eye lens *136*, *137*
Flare 133, *133*
Flash photography 14, *15*, 21,
24, *24*, 25, 42, *43*, 70,
170, 171
Flick book 158, *158*, *159*
Fluorescence 22, *22*, 23
Focus
point of 8
soft 34, 106, *106*, 107, 169,
169
Focusing effects 8, 9, *9*, 73
Food photography 56–7, *56*,
57
Framing the image 62, *62*, 81,
84, 97, 108, *109*, 120,
126, 138
Framing prints 174–5, *175*
Freezing movement 42, *43*, 81,
93
Fresnel lens 169

G

Glamour photography 87,
106–7, *106*, *107*
Glass montage 28–9, *28*
Grain effect 34–5, *35*, 206
Greetings cards 165, 166–7,
167, 217
Gum bichromate prints 212,
212, 213

H

Hamilton, David 106
Hand-coloured print 200–1,
201

Hand-made negative 214–15,
214, *215*
Harbour photography 74, *75*
Haze 39, 102, 114
Heads in close-up photography
110–11, *110*
High-contrast effect 206, *207*
High-key photography 120,
120, *121*
High-viewpoint photography
114, *115*
Holiday photography 178, *179*
Horse racing photography
82–3, *82*
Humour 100–1, *100*, *101*

I

Illustrating a theme 118
Illustrative photography
164–5, *164*, *165*
In-focus 8
Industrial photography 94, *95*
Infra-red light 22, 38–9
Instant pictures 150, *151*

J

Junk objects, photographing
62, *62*, *63*

L

Laminating prints 172, *173*
Lamp
black-light 20
photoflood 24, 56, 148
Landscape photography 39,
46, 60–1, *60*, *61*, 78, *87*,
90, *91*, 93, *93*, 102, 129
Lens 136, 168, *168*
box camera 169
close-up 142
fish-eye *136*, *137*
Fresnel 169
hood 133
long-focus 8, 9, 52, 59, 62,
64, *69*, 70, 73, 74, *75*,
76, *77*, 81, *82*, 83, 84,
88, 95, 97, 110, 114,
133, 138, *139*, 140–1,
140, *141*, 156, 160, 169
macro 19, 62, 142, *143*,
208
magnifying-glass *168*, 169
mirror *53*, *140*
telephoto *see* long-focus lens

wide-angle 74, 89, 114,
124, *125*, 128, 133,
136–7, *136*, *137*, 140,
141, 160, 169
zoom 32, 41, 133
Lettering 166, 167, *167*
Life 134
Light
infra-red 22, 38–9
painting with 24–5, *24*
polarized 18–19, *18*, *19*
shooting against 132–3,
133
stroboscopic 20–1, *20*, 21
ultra-violet 22–3, *22*
Lighting
artificial 12, *12*, *13*, 16, *17*,
20, *20*, 21, *21*, 24, *24*,
25, 28, *28*, 29, 30, *31*,
56, 70, 73, 104, 108,
112, *112*, 113, 120, 122,
128, 133, 148, 195
coloured 12, *12*, *13*
Line-sketch print 194–5, *195*
Long-focus lens 8, 9, 52, 59,
62, 64, *69*, 70, 73, 74, *75*,
76, *77*, 81, *82*, 83, 84,
88, 95, 97, 110, 114,
133, 138, *139*, 140–1,
140, *141*, 156, 160, 169
Look 134
Low-key photography 128–9,
128, *129*
Low-viewpoint photography
112, 124, *124*, 125

M

Macro lens 19, 62, 142, *143*,
208
Magnifying-glass lens *168*, 169
Manipulating the image
183–217
Market photography 84, *85*
Mirror lens *53*, *140*
Mirrors 10, *11*, 22, 170
Montage
glass 28–9, *28*, 192
printing 166, 190–1, *191*,
215
Mood, use of colour for 118,
119
Moon, Sarah 106
Mosaic, contact sheet 156–7,
157
Mounting prints 166, 172,
173, 174–5, *175*

Movement 14, *15*, 40–1, *41*, 142
  creation of 158, *159*
  freezing 42, *43*, 81, 93
Moving-light technique 24, *24*, 25
Multiple image exposure 21, 36–7, *37*, 64
Multiprism 171
Muybridge, Edweard 42

N

Natural history close-up photography 142, *143*, *144*
Negative, hand-made 214–15, *214*, *215*
Nude, abstract *17*, 148–9, *149*

O

Optics 168–9, *168*, *169*
Out-of-focus 8, 9, *9*
Over-exposure 34, 36, 45, *45*, 102, 120, 123, 129, 131, 146, 154, 188, 191
Overlay 172, *173*

P

Panning technique 41, *41*, 42, *43*, 156
Panoramic photography 160, *161*
Paper
  background 148
  bromide 168, 189, 192, 196
  colour base 195
  photographic 35, 158, 188, 206
  reversal 168–9
  screen 30, *31*, 56, 112
  sensitized 212–13
  textured 184
  tinted 216
Paris Match 134
Park photography 86–7, *86*, *87*
Pattern *79*, 116–17, *116*, *117*, 138, *139*, 142, *144*, 198, *199*, 206, 215
People, photographing 72–3, *72*, *73*, 78, 80–1, *82*, *83*, 84, *85*, 86, 90, 148–9, *149*
  glamour *see* Glamour

photography
  working 72–7, *72*, *73*
Perspective 110, 116, 141
Photo-colour dye 200, *201*
Photo-essay 87, 89, 118, 180, *181*, *182*
Photoflood lamp 24, 56, 148
Photogram 192, *193*, 214
Photografik Kit 189
Photo-journalism 134, 137
Photo-linen 198, 210, *211*
Photosensitized aluminium sheet 211
Physiogram *17*, 170–1, *171*
Picture story 73, 87, 89, 90, 93, 134–5, *135*, 152, *153*, 180
Picture wall, 174, 175, 180
Pinhole camera 168–9, *168*, *169*
Point of focus 8
Polarized light 18–19, *18*, *19*
Portfolio 172, *173*, 180
  box 172, *173*
Portraits 69, 70, *70*, *71*, 73, 87, 90, 110, *110*, *111*, 114, 126, 128, 132, 141
Poster photography 164, 165, 166
Posterization 184–5, *184*, 185
Prints
  on colour base paper 195
  contact 156–7, *157*, 158, 160, 184, 192, *193*, 195, 208, 212
  on different surfaces 198, 210–11, *211*
  display of 172, *173*, 174–5, *175*
  distorted 196–7, *196*, *197*
  framing 174–5, *175*
  gum bichromate 212–13, *212*
  hand-coloured 200–1, *201*
  laminating 172, *173*
  line-sketch 194–5, *195*
  mounting 166, 172, *173*, 174, 175, *175*
  patterns 198, *199*
  portfolio 172, *173*, 180
  presentation 172, *173*
  solarized 188–9, *188*, *189*, 217, *217*
  toning black and white 195, 216–17, *217*
Projector, slide *see* Slide projector

Pseudo-solarization 189, *189*
Punch and pin register board 184, 185, *185*
Push-processing techniques 34, 35, 97, 107

R

Railway photography 88, 89, *89*
Red-eye effect 70
Reflected image (*see also* Mirrors) 66, *67*
Reflector 56, 70, 148
Registration 184, 185, *185*
Romantic glamour photography
  see Glamour photography

S

Sabbatier effect 188, 189
Screen
  canvas 186
  diffusing 148
  silk 186
  texture *28*, *111*, 186–7, *186*, *187*, 192
  tracing-paper 30, *31*, 56, 112
Seaside photography 78, *79*
Shadow 104, *104*, *105*, 110
Shooting against the light 132–3, *133*
Shop window photography 64, *65*
Shutter speed 14, 42, *43*, 81, 93
Silhouette 112–13, *112*, *113*, 124, 146, 192
Silk screen 186
Silver halide emulsion 211, *211*
Simplicity 126, *126*, *127*
Sky photography 146, *147*
Slide duplication 36, 205, 208, *208*, *209*
Slide projection, back 29, 30, *31*, 192
Slide projection effects 16, *17*
Slide sandwich 167, 204–5, *205*
SLR camera 9, 37, 133, 136, 142, 168, 208
Snowscape 102, 176, *177*
Soft focus 34, 106–7, *106*, *169*, *169*

Solarization 188–9, *188*, *189*, 217, *217*
Special assignments 145–82
Star-burst effect 10, 171
Step-by-step sequence 73, 87, 90, 162–3, *162*, *163*
Still-life photography 10, *11*, 30, *31*, 56–7, *56*, *57*, 114
Street life photography 68–9, *68*, *69*, 84, *85*
Strobe effects 20–1, *20*, *21*
Style and approach 99–144
Subject idea file 51–98
Sunsets 154–5, *155*

T
Telephoto lens *see* Lens, long-focus
Texture 45, 79, 116, 122–3, *122*, *123*, 138, *139*, 142, *144*, 149, 192, 206, 215
screen 28, 111, 186–7, *186*, *187*, 192
Time exposure 24, *24*, 25, 48–9, *49*, 170

Tone separation 184–5, *184*, *185*
Toner, chemical 210, 216, 217
Toning black and white prints 195, 216–17, *217*
Town photography 54–5, *54*, *55*, 60–1, *60*, *61*, 68–9, *68*, *69*
Tracing-paper screen 30, *31*, 56, 112
Transparency *see* Slide
Tree photography 58, 59
Tri-colour photography 32, *33*
Tripod 21, 24, 30, 32, 41, 52, 54, 56, 62, 88, 122, 138, 141, 142, 156, 158, 160, 170

U
Ultra-violet light 22–3, *22*
Under-exposure 35, 38, 45, *45*, 97, 102, 123, *129*, 131, 132, *133*, 154, 176, 206
Urban photography 54–5, *54*, *55*, 60–1, *60*, *61*, 68–9, *68*, *69*

V
Viewfinder camera 9, 122, 124, 142

W
Waterways photography 92–3, *92*, *93*
Weather photography 102, *103*, 129, 146, *147*, 154–5, *155*, 176, *177*
Wide-angle lens 74, 89, 114, 124, *125*, 128, 133, 136–7, *136*, *137*, 140, 141, 160, 169
Wildlife photography 52, *53*, 76, *76*, *77*, 93
Worm's-eye view photography 124–5, *124*, *125*

Z
Zoo photography 76, *76*, *77*
Zoom lens 32, 41, 133

Acknowledgements

The author would like to express his thanks to the following people:

Pat Busselle who typed the manuscript.
Paul Russell and Julien Busselle who sowed the seeds of the idea for the book.
Peter Cogram and John Miller for their enthusiasm and assistance with the photography and darkroom work.
Hilary Dickinson and Chris White for their tireless efforts and patience in putting the whole thing together.
Robert Adkinson and Clare Howell for their encouragement and supervision.

All the photographs in the book were taken by Michael Busselle, the author, with the exception of the following:
55 (right) Michael Freeman
98 (bottom) J. Zimmermann/Frank W. Lane
139 (all) Elizabeth Hollingsworth